AN INTRO...
GR...

AN INTRODUCTION TO GRAPHOLOGY

Ellen Cameron

Aquarian/Thorsons
An Imprint of HarperCollinsPublishers

The Aquarian Press
An Imprint of HarperCollins*Publishers*
77–85 Fulham Palace Road,
Hammersmith, London W6 8JB

Published by The Aquarian Press 1989
3 5 7 9 10 8 6 4

A catalogue record for this book
is available from the British Library

ISBN 0 85030 818 6

Typeset by Harper Phototypesetters
Limited, Northampton
Printed in Great Britain by
HarperCollinsManufacturing Glasgow

Contents

To Ian

Introduction

This course is designed to promote a wider interest in graphology, introducing those with little or no previous knowledge of the subject to the science of interpreting character from handwriting.

Graphology is by no means a modern study. Many centuries ago the Ancient Chinese showed an interest in the psychology of handwriting, recognizing in those early times a link between writing and character traits. In Europe during the Middle Ages the art of writing was mainly pursued and taught by monks. By the thirteenth century writing was becoming more widely practised by educated people. But the earliest work written on the relationship between handwriting and personality was compiled by Dr Baldo, an Italian Doctor of Medicine and Philosophy in the early seventeenth century.

The origin of modern graphology comes from France. The Abbé Jean Michon, a graphologist with wide interests who published novels and books on many subjects, formulated from research and personal experience the main principles of graphology. The term 'graphology', derived from the Greek words 'grapho' and 'logos' meaning respectively 'I write' and 'doctrine' or 'theory', was introduced by the Abbé in 1871.

In the later nineteenth century the German school were investigating a system of graphology based on psychology and physiology in relationship to other characteristics. Dr Ludwig Klages their leading researcher became the first person to form the complete theory of graphology.

Continental graphology was brought to England by Shooling who translated into English an important work of Crépieux-Jamin, a talented pupil of the Abbé Jean Michon. In his book Crépieux-Jamin stressed the importance of studying handwriting in all its aspects, not by individual traits. Between 1926 and 1928 Robert Saudek, a handwriting expert and linguist from Prague, published two books in English based on the German theory of graphology.

In 1939 another Continental graphologist Hans Jacoby came to this country publishing *'Analysis of Handwriting'*, an excellent book 'introducing for the first time a graphological method which is based on the science of the expression of movement' and which, as the author also states, 'Tries to point out to parents, educators, medical men, psychologists, criminologists and everyone who is interested in the psychological investigation of personality the importance of a scientifically executed analysis of handwriting and to show what can be expected of graphology'.

Several of our famous writers and artists including William Shakespeare, Edgar Allen Poe, Sir Walter Scott, the poet Byron, the painter Gainsborough and also Disraeli the politician, have taken a keen interest in handwriting. But Stephen Collett was the first Englishman to study in detail the relationship between handwriting and personality. His findings were published in 1823.

Every nation has its own individual style of writing and although all handwriting shows some national characteristics, each person's handwriting is unique to the individual in the same way as no two people have identical fingerprints. Graphology can be a fascinating hobby or studied more seriously. In Europe it has been taught as an academic study at universities for many years and is acknowledged as a science in the United States.

In Britain graphology is rapidly becoming established as a science. In the past it has sometimes been falsely associated with the pseudo-sciences, as a form of fortune-telling. Handwriting analysis is not a means of foretelling the future but can indicate the character traits and potential of the writer at the time of writing. The Graphology Society and the British Institute of Graphologists have done much to publicize the true definition of graphology and fields in which it can be used advantageously.

In several countries scientific graphology has been practised for many years as a backing-up factor in personnel selection, vocational guidance, police investigations and other spheres, and in Britain it is now more widely applied in this capacity.

It is not possible to assess accurately the age or sex of a person from their writing. Some old people remain vital and young at heart, whilst there are young people who are old for their years.

Likewise some women have masculine traits and there are men with feminine characteristics. For these reasons the age and sex of a writer are revealed to the graphologist prior to analysis.

We are not always as we seem. Many obvious character traits show up in our handrwriting but there are also hidden traits in our personality, not apparent to others, which can be revealed by the science of graphology. It is important to remember, when studying handwriting, that snap analyses must not be made by assessing only one or a few features of the writing. All aspects must be taken into consideration before a character 'portrait' can be drawn up.

Materials Required for the Course:

1 six-inch ruler marked in centimetres and inches.
1 Protractor.
1 Magnifying glass.

1. The Three Zones

Handwriting is divided into three zones; the upper, the middle and the lower. The upper zone contains the upper strokes and loops of letters, such as 'b', 'd' and 'l'. Small letters, for example 'a', 'c', 'e' and 's' occupy the middle zone, while the lower strokes and loops of letters like 'f', 'g' and 'y' are contained in the lower zone.

When we start school we are taught the 'copy-book' form of writing, which can be described as balanced writing, each zone measuring approximately 3mm. The letters are formed individually at first and at a later stage letters in a word are joined together. (See Figure 1.)

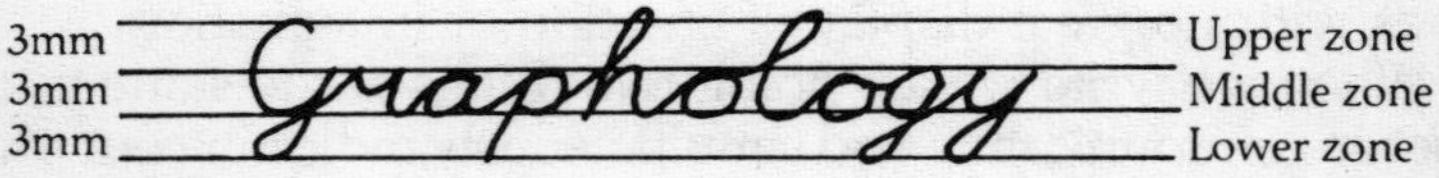

3mm		Upper zone
3mm	*Graphology*	Middle zone
3mm		Lower zone

Figure 1

The writing slopes moderately to the right with every 'm' and 'n' showing an arched formation at the top, which is termed 'arcade'. All the letters are legible with i-dots placed directly overhead and t-bars evenly distributed about three-quarters of the way up the stem. (See Figure 2.)

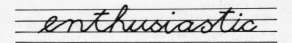

Figure 2

Although children attempt to copy their teacher's example of handwriting careful examination of their work shows that in most cases some degree of change has been made in the size, slant, letter formation, or other aspect of the writing. For example, a child may have a natural inclination to slant letters to the left or upright, while another may have difficulty in keeping the size of their writing within the zones. So even in early school-days character traits are beginning to show in our writing. The aggressive child's handwriting will differ from that of a happy, placid, easygoing youngster, while the emotions of anxious or nervous children will be reflected in their writing. Likewise laziness and carelessness can also be detected at an early stage.

As our character forms so we develop our own individual style of writing. Over the years some people's writing will show many changes while others differ only slightly from the copy-book form during the whole course of their lives. The latter are usually comparatively well-balanced people, showing no exceptional talents but leading ordinary, steady, well-regulated lives with no great display of emotion or imagination.

When we write we are doing two things at the same time. We are communicating and simultaneously indicating our own personality. Human personality can be divided into three areas, the mind, the soul and the body, which in graphology are represented respectively by the upper, middle and lower zones.

The upper zone is the area of intellectual and spiritual qualities. The sphere of meditation, reflection, aspirations and striving. When the upper zone is emphasized the writer's intellectual attributes are dominant. Full rounded upper loops indicate imagination and emotion, lean or thin loops show lack of imagination, sometimes excessive rationalization, and no loops logical thinking without fantasies.

The middle zone is the area in which one's likes, dislikes and personal adaptability to everyday life are expressed. The middle zone is emphasized when the social scene and everyday occurrences are of major importance to the writer. A small middle zone can be an indication of inferiority feelings, but it is also a sign of intellectual clarity, depending on other features in the writing. Einstein and many other people of great intellect show a small middle zone in their writing. In this zone 'fullness', which means the letters circumscribe a larger surface area than prescribed in the copy-book form, suggests a warm, caring personality, whereas a 'lean' middle zone, which implies the letters take up less space than allowed for in the copy-book form indicates the opposite tendencies. The writer is of a less genial disposition, being more down-to-earth in his approach to life.

The foundation of our personality lies in the lower zone. When this sphere is emphasized the practical, material or instinctual side of life is dominant.

Extremely small or stunted lower lengths of the letters 'g' and 'y' usually imply a suppression of instincts, in which case the writer's drive may be channelled into other spheres, such as an all absorbing everyday activity or some preoccupying intellectual pursuit.

Full lower loops suggest a strong, active imagination which could suggest creative or artistic tendencies, or take the form of wishes or dreams about sex, money or material interests which may not necessarily be realized. A lean lower zone can be the sign of a realist, a down-to-earth type of person, someone with a good business head or preoccupied with material interests.

In handwriting the zones can be compared to a tree. The upper zone being similar to the branches reaching upwards. The middle zone like the trunk, the central part of our lives. The lower zone, like the roots holding the tree in place, is the foundation of our personality.

We have seen in Figure 1 that the three zones in the copy-book form of writing are balanced, each measuring approximately 3mm, but in many cases as a person's character develops this balance is no longer retained. Whichever zone is emphasized the qualities of that sphere will be dominant in the writer's personality.

By studying examples 2-8 of the word 'flap', in Figure 3, it can be seen how the character traits of the writer are indicated by various combinations in the size of the zones.

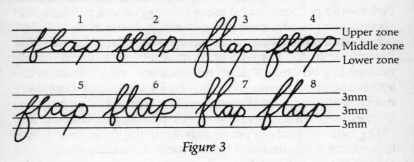

Figure 3

The balanced writing of the copy-book form in example 1 suggests a contented personality, possessing inner harmony. A person with no exceptional talents, but an average to good all-rounder.

Example 2 shows a large middle zone with small upper and lower lengths. Such writers live in the 'here and now', their interests lying mainly in the social involvement of everyday life. They are usually self-confident, at home in social gatherings, being at their best when amongst other people. Boredom can be a problem as there appear to be few intellectual aspirations, inclinations to make money or undertake absorbing practical or material interests.

The writer of example 3 shows domination in the upper and lower zones at the expense of the middle zone. Although the writer possesses the inner qualities to strive with ambition, the lack of inner strength, as suggested by a comparatively small middle zone, may create difficulties in sustaining an otherwise strong personality.

In example 4 the middle and lower zones are large with a small upper zone. The writer is self-confident, wrapped up in everyday life, enjoying social involvement. This side of the personality is supported by instinctual and/or materialistic drives, but there appear comparatively few intellectual ambitions.

Example 5 shows emphasis in the lower zone with an average middle zone and small upper zone. This is the writing of a down-to-earth person who takes a normal interest in everyday life but is not so involved in intellectual pursuits.

In example 6 the upper and middle zones are large and the lower zone small. This writer is ambitious with high intellectual aspirations, has plenty of self-confidence and takes an active part in everyday activities, but the foundations of the personality are weak.

Example 7 shows a large upper zone with small middle and lower zones. This writer is intellectually active with high aspirations and would strive hard to fulfil ambitions, but has little social self-confidence or interest in the everyday social scene and no firm roots to the personality. So although much may be achieved by determination the qualities of the middle and lower zones could deter greater accomplishments.

In example 8 the middle and lower zones are average with a large upper zone. Here the writer would most likely take a normal interest in everyday social activities, and have firm roots to his/her personality. The writer's intelligence and ambitions are sustained by a balance between the middle and lower zones.

To gain a better understanding of this course in graphology the reader should acquire several samples of handwriting and first examine them separately for the features listed in each chapter, then work through the exercises at the end of the chapter.

Exercise 1

1 Measure vertically in millimetres the average height of each of the three zones in several different samples of handwriting.

2 Are the three zones balanced? If so is the writing similar in size to the copy-book form each zone measuring approximately 3mm, or is the writing larger or smaller?

3 If the zones are not balanced which zone or zones show dominance? What qualities are represented by these zones?

4 Comparing the samples of handwriting with Figure 3, do the combinations in the size of the zones resemble any of those shown in examples 1-8? If so, what interpretation would you give for this aspect of the handwriting?

5 What could be the significance of:

    a A small middle zone.

    b An emphasized middle zone.

    c Stunted lower lengths of letters 'g' and 'y'.

    d Full lower lengths.

6 Which zone represents the roots of the personality?

2. Size and Width

Size

By looking at several samples of handwriting it will be seen that there are many different styles of writing, although most of us were taught the copy-book form at school. Possibly one of the earliest changes from the school form is in the size, which may be enlarged or made smaller. The absolute size of handwriting is the combined size of the upper, middle and lower lengths. In the copy-book form this is approximately 9mm.

The dominant absolute size of a sample of handwriting can be assessed by taking vertical measurements from the tips of the upper zone to the depths of the lower zone. For example in Figure 6, a sample of small writing, the height of the letter 'f' in the word 'for' covering all three zones, or a measurement taken from the top of the letter 'h' to the base of the letter 'g' in the word 'daughters'. In this instance the absolute size of the small writing is about 5mm but some writing can measure as little as 2mm and still remain legible. Should the measurements of size be markedly irregular throughout the script, causing difficulty in assessing a dominant absolute size, this usually denotes the presence of strain in the writer.

The relative size of handwriting is the size of the upper, middle and lower zones in relation to each other. Various combinations in the size of the three zones and possible interpretations have been dealt with in Chapter 1.

In medium writing (see Figure 4) the absolute size is in the region of 9mm (approximately 8-10mm), with writing classified as large or small being either over or under the medium measurements.

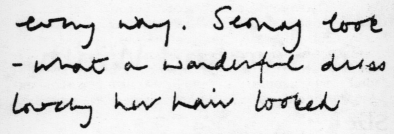

Figure 4: Medium script

Characteristics of Large Writers

Writers of large script have a natural inclination to enlarge their writing (see Figure 5). It is difficult for them to do otherwise. Such people are more subjective than objective. They are generally enthusiastic and self-confident needing plenty of space to express themselves, not liking to be confined or restricted in any way. They may be ambitious but not always well-disciplined, sometimes in their enthusiasm they become carried away with their notions and tend to neglect the realities of life.

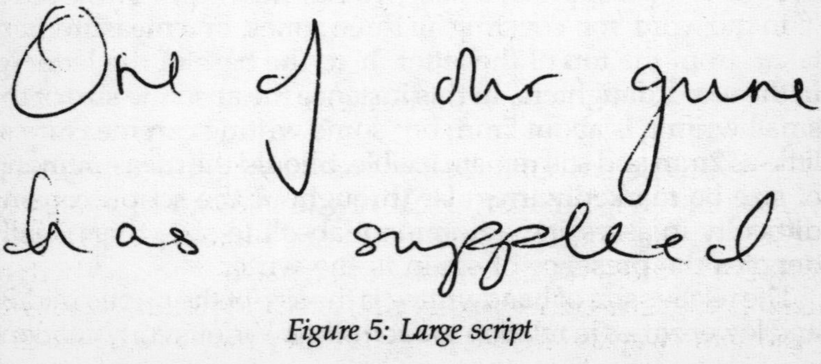

Figure 5: Large script

The larger the script the more these tendencies will apply to the writer, but as all traits in handwriting have both a positive and a negative interpretation other features in the writing must also be taken into consideration.

Backed by intelligence, will-power, drive and other positive features portrayed in the script, the writer's desire to achieve great things has a good basis for success. But on the other hand, if the large writing shows negative traits, such as lack of discipline or realism, inconsideration, and a tendency to pose, the writer's wish for success may not materialize but rather turn in on the writer who would possibly become boastful and swollen-headed. Many people in the public eye, like pop stars and celebrities who enjoy being in the limelight, tend to enlarge their writing.

Characteristics of Small Writers
Unlike large writers, the writers of small script have a natural inclination to make their writing smaller (see Figure 6). Again they may find difficulty in doing otherwise.

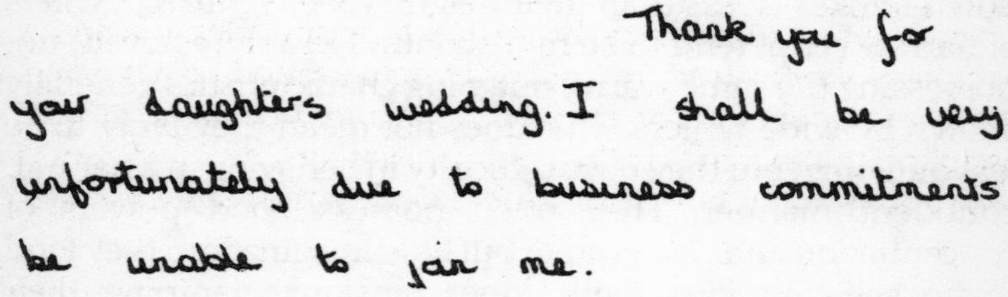

Thank you for your daughters wedding. I shall be very unfortunately due to business commitments be unable to join me.

Figure 6: Small script

These people are often modest, not having the same need of space for self-expression, preferring to think and operate on a smaller scale. Small writers tend to be more realistic, well-disciplined, thoughtful, accurate and reliable. They are better suited to scientific and technical work, not caring for the limelight in the same way as large writers. But they may also be small-minded, lacking in self-confidence, and at times prone to inferiority feelings, being more reserved and submissive.

Width

The width or breadth of handwriting can be medium, narrow or wide. Width is measured in the middle zone and is associated with the writer's emotional adjustment to everyday life. It is measured in millimetres as the distance between the down-strokes of a letter; this is most easily seen and measured in the letters 'n', 'm' and 'u'. Width is *not* the distance between the letters themselves. This is termed Secondary Width, and is dealt with under that heading.

Width is described as medium when, for example, in a letter 'n' the distance between the two downstrokes measures the same as their height. (See Figure 7.) Writers of medium width and similarly those with medium sized writing, many of whom fall into this category, show a medium or average adaptability to everyday life. They could be described as moderates.

Writing is termed narrow when the distance between the down-strokes is less than their height. (See Figure 8.) Writers of narrow script tend to be more controlled and reserved, not possessing the same warm, outgoing characteristics generally shown by wide writers. This does not mean they *prefer* to be less outgoing, but they have difficulty in behaving in a natural, confident manner. They often possess good powers of concentration and observation but little imagination. they tend to be self-conscious, with inner tensions cramping their personality. Narrow writers are also capable of carrying a sense of economy to the extreme.

Writing is termed wide when the distance between the down-strokes is greater than their height. (See Figure 9.) Wide or broad writers show a desire to expand their writing laterally. They are usually spontaneous, frequently self-indulgent and not always very well-disciplined, but they are well-adjusted emotionally to everyday life, not having the same degree of tension as writers of a narrow script.

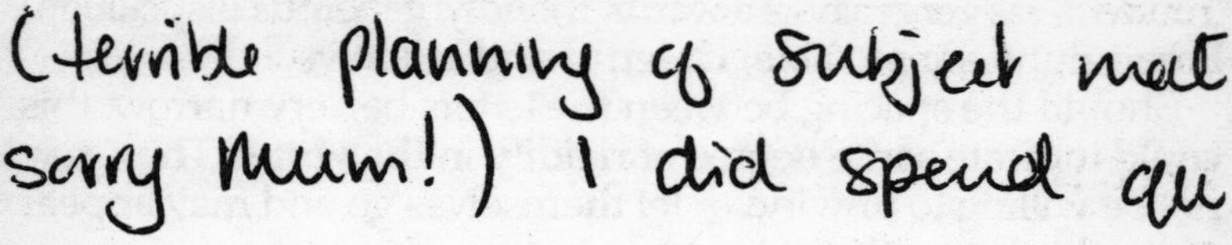

*(terrible planning of subject mat
sorry mum!) I did spend an*

Figure 7: Medium width

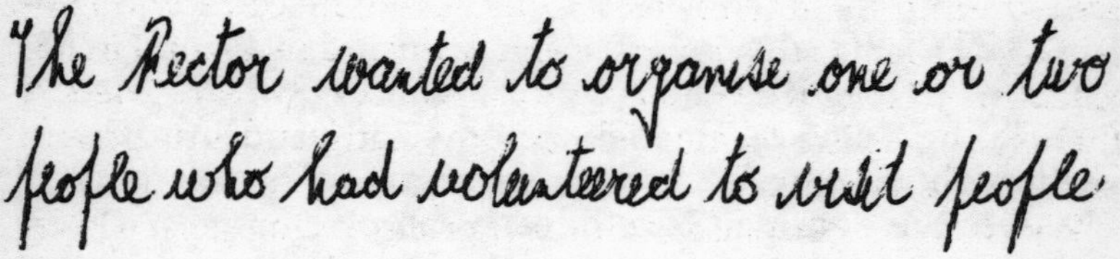

*The Rector wanted to organise one or two
people who had volunteered to visit people.*

Figure 8: Narrow script

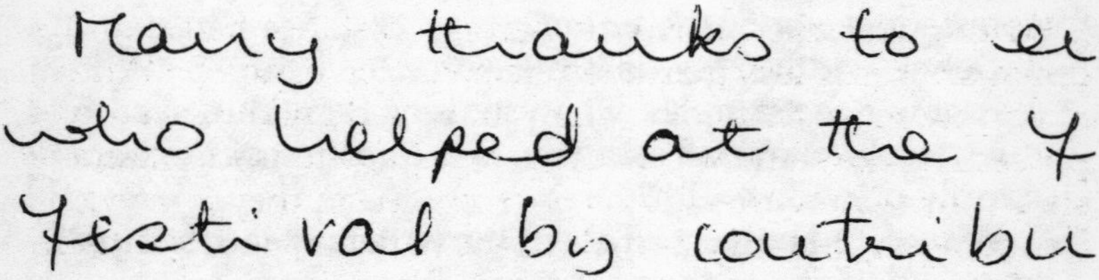

*Many thanks to a
who helped at the y
Festival by contribu*

Figure 9: Wide script

Secondary Width

This is the distance between the letters in a word, *not* the width of the individual letters. When the writing is wide, there is a spread-out appearance, the writer needing space for self-expression, most likely enjoying travel and outgoing activities.

The writer is generally of a warm, friendly, generous disposition, broad-minded, sociable, cheerful and talkative.

Should the spacing between the letters be very narrow, this could indicate some degree of rigidity in the writer. They may not be willing to unwind or let themselves go and may appear of a cold disposition.

Exercise 2

1 Taking several measurements of absolute size throughout the script, in different samples of handwriting, assess the dominant size in each sample.

2 Do the samples classify as medium, large or small writing?

3 What could be learned about the writers from this aspect of their writing? If there were wide variations in the individual measurement of size in a sample what would you deduce about the writer?

4 Define width. How is it measured?

5 Examine the samples of handwriting for width, in each case taking an overall estimate. Is the writing of medium narrow or wide width?

6 What could be learned about the writers of each sample from the width of their writing?

7 How does the definition 'secondary width' differ from that of 'width'?

8 Examine the samples for secondary width and in each case suggest possible interpretations.

3. Legibility and Slant

Legibility

A dictionary definition of 'legible' is 'easy to read'. Writing is a means of communication with other people and, when legible, is easily and correctly read. Most handwriting is reasonably legible, the gist of the script being understood even where a writer's individual expression of character has modified some letter formations.

A good degree of legibility (see Figure 10) suggests a straightforward, sincere person, reliable and considerate of

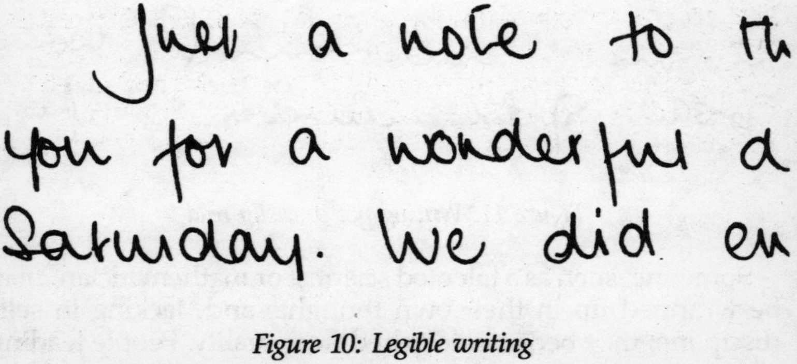

Figure 10: Legible writing

others. One who wishes to impart a message with no attempt to conceal facts. Good legibility can also imply lack of individuality or strong impulses, indicating the type of person who adapts easily and conventionally, having little desire for self-expression.

There is yet another aspect of legibility, fortunately not so frequently encountered, that of a crafty type attempting to hide their true nature, for some iniquitous reason, behind a guise of conventional writing. Other features in the writing should confirm or refute such an interpretation.

Illegibility

If the reason for writing is to communicate with others, when writing is illegible this purpose would appear to be defeated. Why then is some handwriting illegible? (See Figure 11.) It could be the writer lacks consideration for others and once having put pen to paper no longer cares whether the message is understood or not.

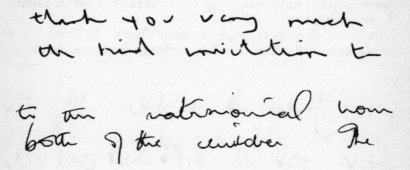

Figure 11: Writing not so easily read

Someone, such as a talented scientist or mathematician, may be wrapped up in their own thoughts and, lacking in self-discipline, may become detached from reality. People leading busy lives may scarcely find time to scribble what becomes an illegible message before dashing off to their next appointment. Or those whose thoughts fly ahead faster than they can be recorded by hand tend to produce illegible script. In all these cases of illegibility there is a common factor — lack of consideration for the recipient. But there are also people who, while suffering acute anxiety, have difficulty in controlling their writing, which deteriorates becoming illegible. In such cases other signs of anxiety will be present in the writing.

Legibility, as with all handwriting characteristics, must not be judged solely on its own merits, but be taken into consideration along with all other features of the writing.

Slant

Handwriting has been referred to as brain writing; messages transmitted from the brain being recorded by the hand. In the Western world writing starts at the left side of the page and progresses across the sheet towards the right, thus as the writing moves forward the left becomes the writer's past, the position reached the present, and ahead lies the future towards which the writer is advancing.

A perpendicular line drawn from the upper zone, through the baseline, and into the lower zone forms a division between influences of self and the past to the left, and the pull of the outside world and the future to the right. (See Figure 12.)

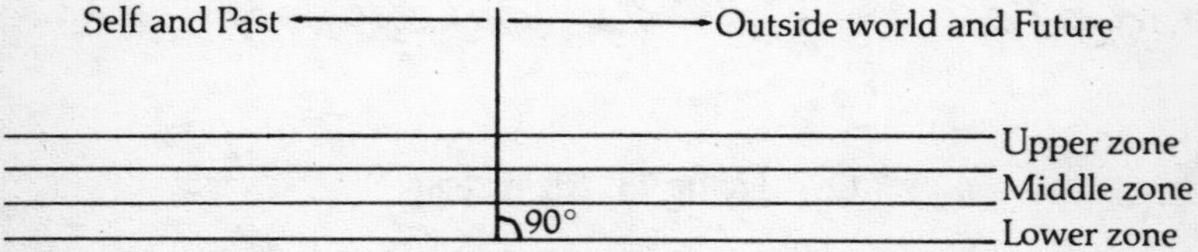

Self and Past ◄─────── │ ──────► Outside world and Future

Upper zone
Middle zone
90°
Lower zone

Figure 12

The slant of the handwriting is an indication of a writer's feelings and attitude to other people and the outside world. There are three main slants: to the right, upright, and to the left, although the slant of some handwriting fluctuates throughout the script, showing a mixture of two or all three slants.

Right slant

A slant to the right (see Figure 13) represents extroversion. It is the slant most commonly found in handwriting and taught at school in the copy-book form of writing.

There are various degrees of right slant. The average is in the region of 30° to the right of the perpendicular line. To make this measurement the centre of the base of the protractor is placed at the 90° position on the baseline of the letter to be measured. The ruler is then laid along the slant of the letter to the outside measurement on the protractor. The measurement is generally easier to make if the slant is followed along the length of a letter reaching into the upper zone such as '1'. So if the slant is 30° to the right of the perpendicular line the ruler would lie across the 120° mark on the protractor.

Measuring slant in this way shows the degree of deviation from the perpendicular line position of 90°, which could be described as zero slant.

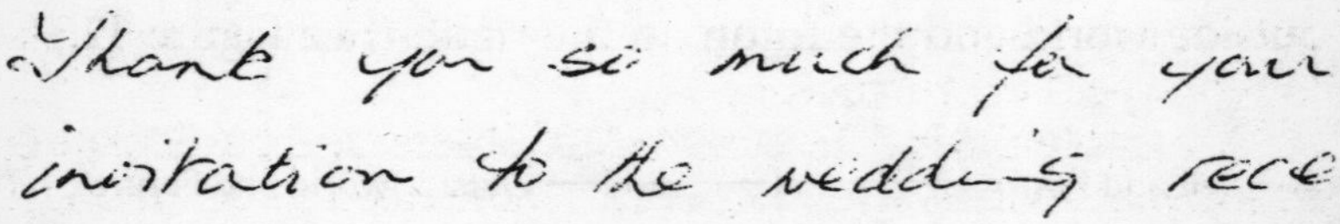

Thank you so much for your invitation to the wedding rece

Figure 13: Right slant

Writers of a medium slant to the right are usually of a friendly disposition, outgoing, affectionate and demonstrative. They enjoy the company of others and social events, being best suited to working with other people. They are well adapted to occupations such as social work, sales representatives, acting etc. But whereas the writers of an average right slant are usually well-balanced, being prepared to both give and take, the greater the slant leans to the right and the more the writing looks as if it is falling over, the more the writer is dependent on and influenced by the opinions of others.

Upright Slant

Slant can be described as upright when the writing is perpendicular to the baseline or with only an occasional slight deviation to the left or right. (See Figure 14.)

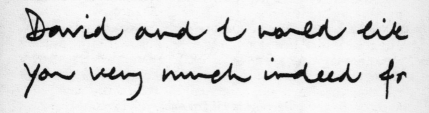

Figure 14: Upright slant

Upright writers are usually of a more reserved disposition, not readily showing their emotions, tending to be more independent and self-assured. They are frequently charming, self-possessed people capable of remaining calm in times of crisis and able to work well under pressure.

Although enjoying the company of others, and participating in social acitivities, there is not the same need to be amongst people as with right-slanted writers. Neither are they so easily influenced, being guided more by their own judgements and opinions.

Writers of an upright slant showing leadership qualities, such as the positive traits of ambition and intelligence, are likely to do well in executive positions bearing responsibility. They are also, taking other qualities into consideration, well suited to working efficiently on their own or in comparative isolation, not having the same need for company as people with a right slant.

Left Slant
A slant to the left (see Figure 15) represents introversion. An average left slant is approximately 30° left of the perpendicular line, being measured in a similar manner to that of an average right slant, registering in the region of 60° outside measurement on the protractor.

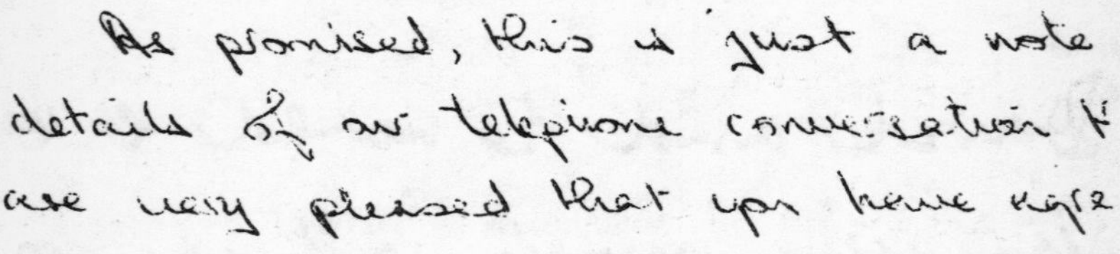

As promised, this is just a note
details of our telephone conversation &
*are very pleased that you have no***

Figure 15: Left slant

Writers of a medium left slant, although frequently talented people, particularly in creative fields, tend to underestimate their ability. They are often shy and sensitive, hiding their feelings behind a mask of reserve. Many artists and poets write with a left slant.

Left-slanted writers tend to hold back their opinions rather than call attention to themselves. Unlike right-slanted people they experience more difficulty in relaxing and mixing freely with others and at times may experience feelings of isolation from the outside world. They tend to adopt a cautious and defensive attitude which could give the false impression of a cold and uncaring nature.

The stronger the slant to the left, the more introverted the writer. So as the slant recedes from the right to the left the less outgoing and more reserved the personality becomes. An extreme left slant is often the sign of great reserve and detachment from reality and everyday life. A slant to the left sometimes develops during adolescence and may change with maturity.

Fluctuating Slants

Fluctuating slants (see Figure 16) are usually an indication of some degree of emotional instability, the interpretation depending on the combination of slants.

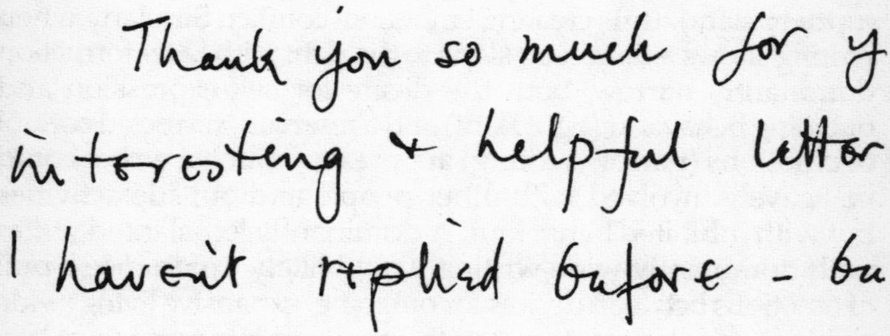

Figure 16: Fluctuating slants

Fluctuating slants can be seen in the writing of some teenagers. When their characters are forming young people are particularly susceptible to outside influences. Subsequently their emotions are pulled in many directions. Fluctuating slants persisting into maturity suggests the presence of inner conflicts. For example, writing showing a combination of upright and slants to the right could indicate a struggle between the writer's desire for self-expression with an outgoing personality (right slant), and the caution of reserve (upright script). Other examples of how inner conflicts can build up are given at the end of the chapter.

When writing shows a mixture of upright, right and left slants the writer is likely to have a changeable disposition. Such people are capable of being moody, excitable, happy, sensitive, reserved, cautious, outgoing etc, in fairly quick succession, showing the characteristics of all three slants. They lack stability and have difficulty in making decisions and judgements. They are, however, well suited to certain types of occupations where a mercurial temperament is often advantageous. Musicians and pop stars are amongst those whose writing shows a mixture of slants.

Counter-Dominant Features

It has already been mentioned how a writer showing a mixture of the upright and right slant could have the desire for self-expression (right slant) but be held back by caution and reserve (upright slant), thus creating emotional conflict. Similarly when writing shows a dominant slope to the right with letter formation dominantly narrow, both the desire for self-expression and outgoing behaviour (right slant) and a reserved, restricted control of emotions (narrow writing) are present. Such a writer could be actively involved with other people and outside activities but with inhibited behaviour. A dominantly left-slanted writer with dominantly wide writing would likely experience a pull of emotions between desires for outgoing, expansive living (wide writing) and the emotional withdrawl and introversion of left-handed writers.

When writing is large with narrow letters, inner conflicts could arise between the wish to participate in expansive enterprises (large writing) and the inherent fear and caution of such actions (narrow writing). This uncertainty could lead to the writer withdrawing from the undertaking.

These are just a few examples of how the presence of inhibiting factors can be revealed from handwriting. Other features, of course, must always be considered before the final character assessment is formed.

Exercise 3

1 Define legibility.
2 Compare several different samples of handwriting for degree of legibility.
3 Give four possible reasons for writing illegibly.
4 Name the three main slants.
5 a Writers of which slant tend to be of a reserved, independent disposition, not easily influenced by others and capable of staying calm in a crisis?
  b Name some likely characteristics of a person with an average (medium) right slant.
  c What is the main character difference between right and left-slanted writers?
6 Name some likely character traits of the writer with an extreme right slant.
7 What type of person would write with a mixture of all three main slants?
8 Give an example of how an inner conflict between a person's desire for self-expression and self-control can be expressed in handwriting.

4. The Form and Degree of Connection

Form of Connection

Form of connection can be defined as the way in which the up-strokes and down-strokes of letters in the middle zone are connected. This is most easily seen in the letters 'n' and 'm', the shape of this connection signifying the writer's general adjustment and personal adaptability to everyday life and the outside world. Sometimes handwriting shows more than one form of connection. Although all forms should be considered when assessing character it is the dominant one which is most clearly related to the writer's personality.

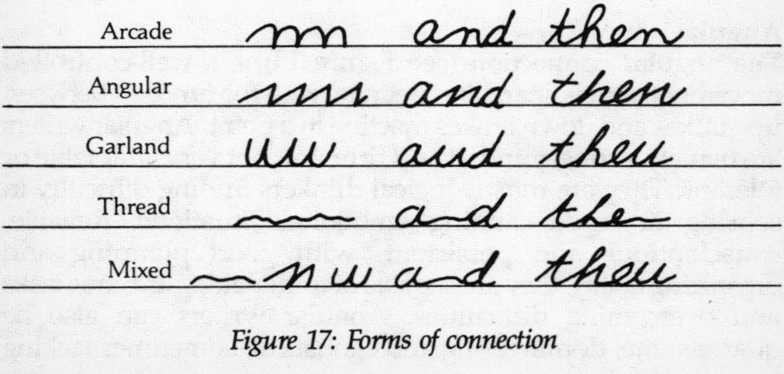

Arcade	*m and then*
Angular	*m and then*
Garland	*m and then*
Thread	*m and the*
Mixed	*n m and then*

Figure 17: Forms of connection

The main forms of connection are the arcade (taught in the copy-book form of writing), angular garland and thread. (See Figure 17.) There is often a close association between garland and thread, the writer using both forms of connection. The same applies between the arcade and angular.

Arcade

The arcade connection (see Figure 18) is a covering up gesture. The tops of the letters 'n' and 'm' are rounded in the form of an arc. Arcade writers are inclined to cover up their thoughts. They tend to be 'private people', rather formal in their behaviour, difficult to get to know easily, keeping their own council and not openly discussing their affairs. However, they are considerate and concerned about the welfare of others.

Artists and musicians often use the arcade form of connection. The higher the arcade, the more artistic the temperament.

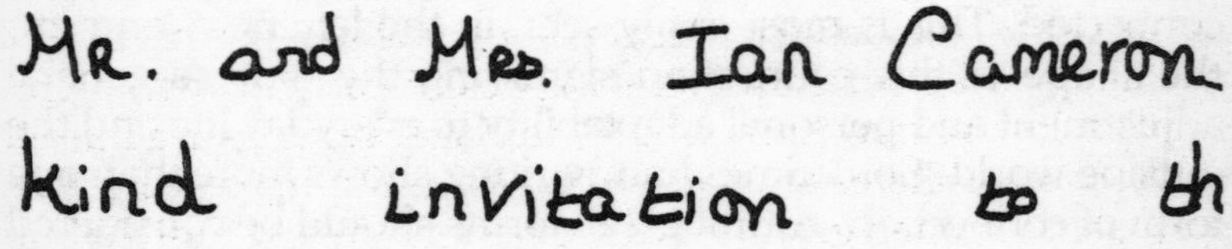

Mr. and Mrs. Ian Cameron
kind invitation to th

Figure 18: Arcade

Angular

The angular connection (see Figure 19) is a well-controlled movement, and is sharp and definite, with the junction between up-strokes and downstrokes meeting in a point. Angular writers are usually strong-minded and firm, but not very adaptable or tolerant. They are mostly logical thinkers finding difficulty in sensing or understanding emotional situations. Reliable, conscientious and persistent, with good planning and organizing ability, they are capable of undertaking arduous tasks and overcoming difficulties. Angular writers can also be quarrelsome, domineering and egotistical, sometimes lacking a sense of humour. Compulsive behaviour is suggested when the angular pattern is both regular and well-defined giving a rugged appearance to the writing.

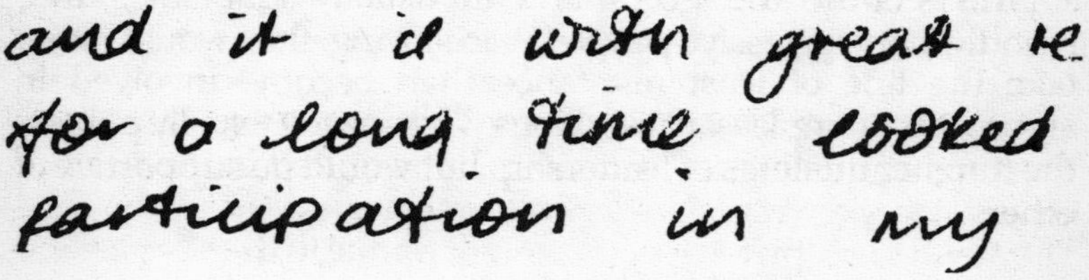

and it id with great re
for a long time cooked
participation in my

Figure 19: Angular

Garland
The garland connection (see Figure 20) is opposed to the arcade, the rounded arc formation of the letter 'n' lying on the baseline of the writing resembling the letter 'u', so that in a word such as 'unusual' the first three letters look like a series of 'u's.

There can be several different types of garland, viz. high, average, low, narrow, spread out — the latter verging on a thread connection. Whereas the arcade is a covering-up gesture, the garland is an open gesture — the emotions are not hidden but

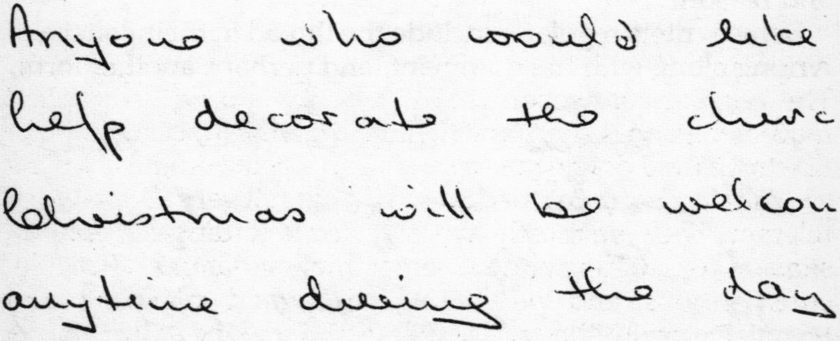

Anyone who would like
help decorate the churc
Christmas will be welcom
anytime during the day

Figure 20: Garland

open and vulnerable to outside influence. A pattern of high garlands can develop through emotional injury, the high receptacle representing stored up resentments which could arouse feelings of depression.

Writers of the average garland are usually adaptable, kind, friendly, non-aggressive people. Peace-loving, they would rather take the line of least resistance than become involved in arguments or unpleasant situations. They do not usually possess the tougher qualities of leadership but would be supportive of others.

Thread

The thread connection (see Figure 21) is the opposite of the angular. Whereas angular writing shows a controlled, somewhat rugged movement, the thread, true to its name, has a flexible, indefinite, snake-like appearance, the letters being stretched out and difficult to decipher.

Writers of a thready script are changeable and adaptable, tending to go the way the wind blows. They like to talk round a subject, attempting to avoid or postpone a definite decision, or may cleverly manipulate à situation to their own advantage. They are frequently creative and versatile possessing intuition and perception, but lacking the stability of inner security, being guided more by their senses and emotions rather than logic and reason.

Some writers regularly include the thread in their pattern of writing along with the dominant, and perhaps another form,

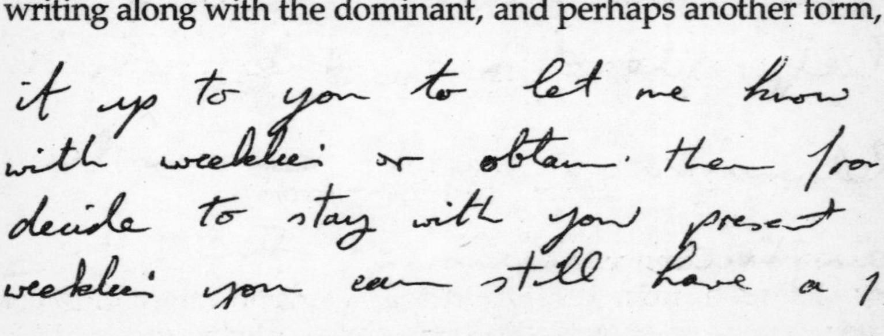

Figure 21: Thread formations

of connection. The influence of the thread is usually one of indecision, a delaying action giving the writer time to consider a situation and perhaps manipulate it to his or her advantage. The thread can also appear temporarily in the writing of overworked people or those under stress, when making decisions becomes difficult. In these cases other signs of stress or strain will be present in the handwriting.

Mixed Forms of Connection

A writer who regularly uses several forms of connection (see Figure 22) will show variability, possessing some characteristics of each of the connections, but the qualities of the dominant one will be most closely linked to the writer's personality, with the others modifying this interpretation to some degree. The distribution of different forms of connection can easily be confirmed by counting the numbers of the various connections present in the sample of handwriting.

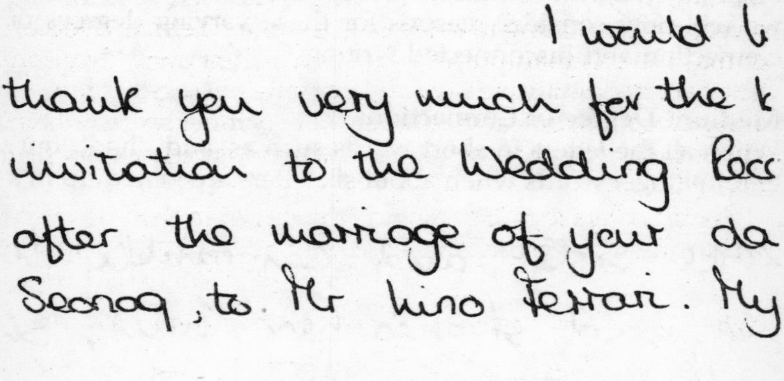

Figure 22: Mixed connections

Degree of Connection

We have seen from the text and illustrations how the connection between the up-strokes and down-strokes of letters in the middle zone; for example, 'n' and 'm' can be arcade, angular, garland or thread. It is the up-strokes which form the connection between letters. How well letters are connected can be linked to a drawbridge between ourselves and the outside world. When the drawbridge is down (the upstrokes present) thoughts flow in logical sequence. The writer's adaptability to others and outside events is good. Should the drawbridge be withdrawn (the upstrokes omitted) then the thought process is interrupted, contact with others is more difficult, and the writer is less adaptable.

So the degree of connection indicates the writer's degree of mental co-ordination and his or her adaptability to other people and the surrounding world. Some writers connect all the letters of each word together in a continual flow, even those letters more difficult to join up. Others not only join all the letters in a word but connect the words together as well. In some cases whole lines of script are joined together. Other writers show breaks in connection between some letters of a word, whilst others present a completely disconnected script. As most of us were originally taught to connect all the letters in a word together we will now consider reasons for these varying degrees of connection and disconnected writing.

Medium Degree of Connection

When all the letters in short words such as 'and', 'had', 'but', and in longer words when about six letters are joined up in a

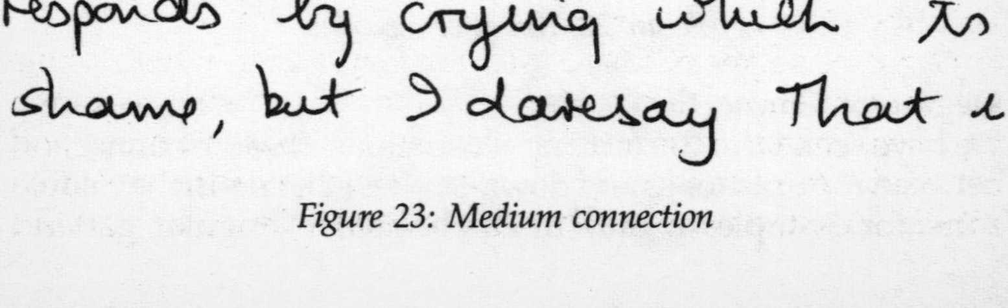

Figure 23: Medium connection

continual movement, the degree of connection is termed 'medium'. A medium degree of connection (see Figure 23) suggests a medium degree of mental and practical adaptability to other people and everyday life.

Well-Connected Writing

A good degree of connection (see Figure 24) is shown when a regular pattern of short words, and in longer words with more than six joined letters, are linked together in a single movement. These writers usually have a sense of purpose with good mental co-ordination, are logical thinkers, and well able to adjust. Friendly, with an easy flow of conversation, they have little difficulty in forming and understanding relationships with others. They are usually good, consistent workers persevering at a task until it is satisfactorily completed, but they may lack initiative, not using much imagination or originality in their undertakings.

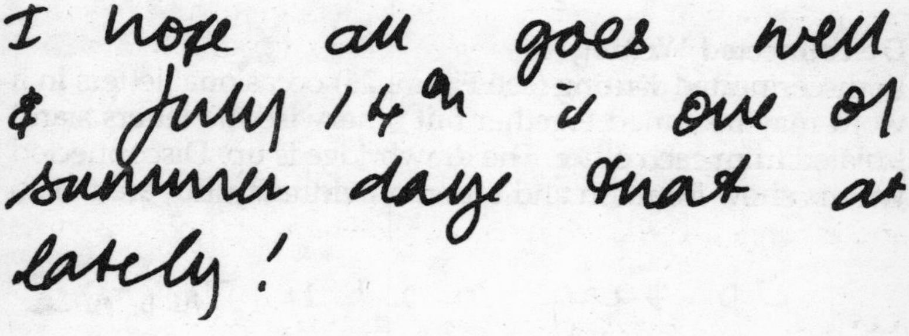

Figure 24: Good connection

Extreme Degree of Connection

An extreme degree of connection (see Figure 25) is where whole words, sentences, and sometimes lines of writing are joined together. Extreme connection shows an over-active mind and can indicate obsessional behaviour. Such writers are often intelligent but so wrapped up in their desire to reach an objective that they are 'blind' to the needs and feelings of others. They can be obstinate, determined and difficult to influence.

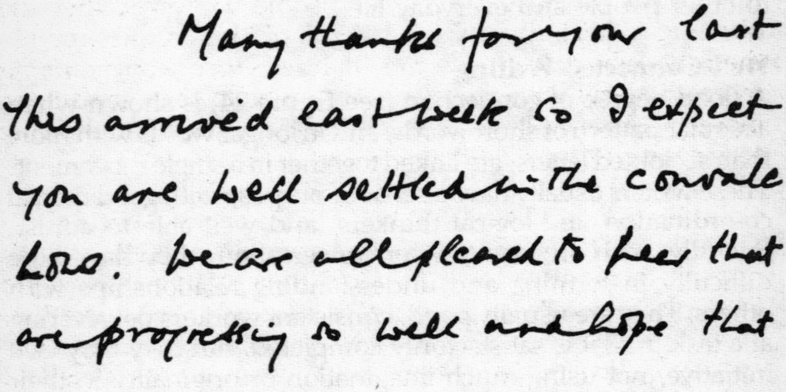

Figure 25: Extreme connection

Disconnected Writing

In disconnected writing (see Figure 26) occasional letters in a word may be joined together but otherwise the letters stand isolated from each other. The drawbridge is up. Disconnected writers show intuition and more individuality, but are not so

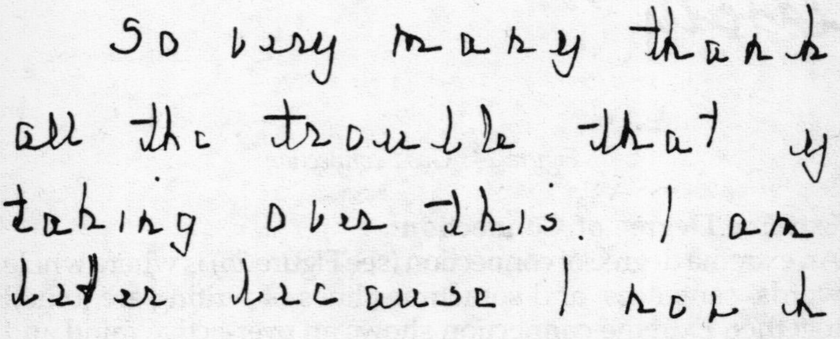

Figure 26: Disconnected scripts

adaptable or co-operative as well-connected writers. They have more difficulty in making or understanding relationships with others, and may appear unsociable, tending to distance themselves mentally from other people. However, they are observant, quick, perceptive and full of ideas. Consequently their thought process is somewhat disjointed, concentrating more on detail than the matter as a whole. They tend to be independent and able to work well on their own, often showing artistic or creative talent.

Combination of Connected and Disconnected Writing

These writers (see Figure 27) possess some characteristics of both connected and disconnected writers, their thoughts tending to flow in sequence with intermittent pauses for consideration; the drawbridge frequently shifting its position. They often show creative ability, intuition, have good powers of reasoning and intelligence, are of an independent disposition and are capable of producing work of outstanding quality. They may also suffer from tensions and show some degree of irritability. Scientists, writers, and those engaged in creative occupations often use a mixed degree of connection in their writing.

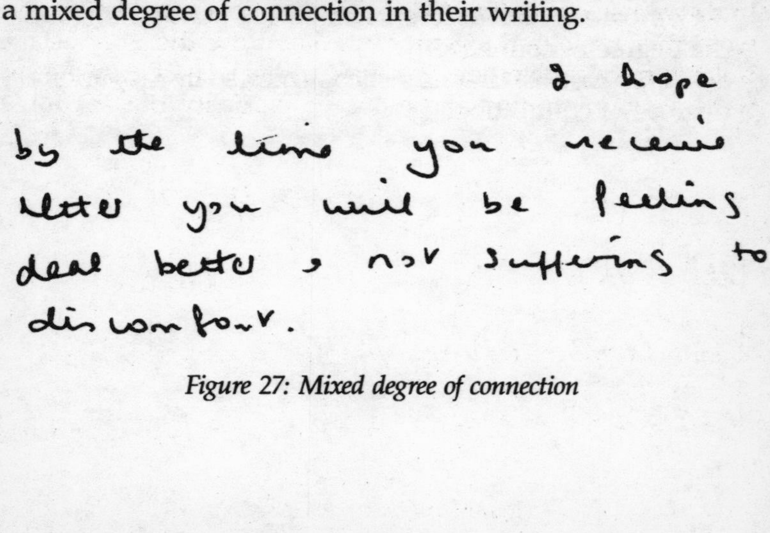

Figure 27: Mixed degree of connection

Exercise 4

1 What are the four main forms of connection?

2 a Examining several different samples of handwriting, decide in each case which form of connection is dominant.

  b Name some characteristics associated with these dominant forms of connection.

3 Do either the angular or thread connection suggest good organizing ability and the capacity for making firm decisions?

4 Give some reasons why writers using the garland connection may not make good leaders.

5 If a sample of handwriting has all the letters of the words connected and also the words joined together in one movement, how would you interpret this degree of connection?

6 What characteristics are suggested by disconnected writing?

7 Compare several different samples of handwriting for the degree of connection.

8 In each case list characteristics suggested by the various degrees of connection.

5. Pressure, Stroke, Regularity, and Rhythm

Pressure

Pressure is created by the muscular grip of the fingertips on the pen and expressed by the hold on the pen and the amount of force directed onto the paper, the degree of pressure exerted being relative to the amount of energy expended by the writer and determined by their personality. The type of pen or nib used will to some degree influence the appearance of pressure, which is more difficult to estimate when a ballpoint pen is used.

When learning to assess pressure it is advisable to examine the strokes of the letters in an original sample of handwriting under a magnifying glass. Pressure can be more easily observed by the difference between light and heavy strokes. Mostly down-strokes are written with heavier pressure than up-strokes.

A simple method of gauging pressure is to find how much indentation has been made by the writing on the back of the page. This can only be detected in original specimens of writing not photocopies. By passing one's fingers over the reverse side of the paper it is possible to feel indentations not easily visible. Marked ridges will show up when very heavy pressure has been applied. It is a sign of light pressure when the reverse side of thinner paper remains smooth with no apparent indentations present.

Pressure can be divided into four main categories: medium, light, heavy and irregular.

Medium Pressure
Most people write with a medium pressure (see Figure 28) denoting a relatively well-balanced personality with good vitality and adaptability to other people and everyday events.

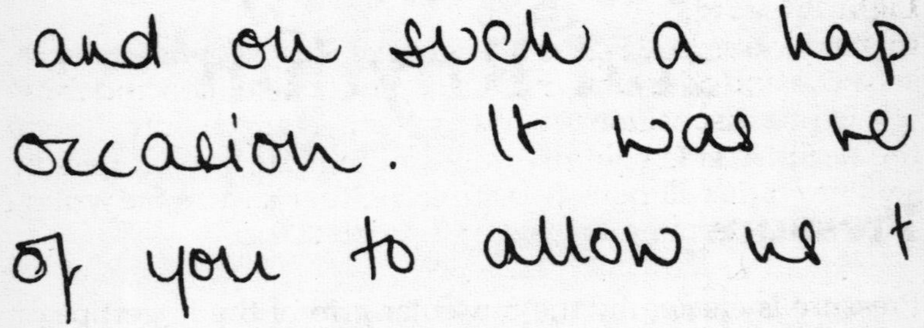

and on such a hap

occasion. It was ve

of you to allow us t

Figure 28: Medium Pressure

Heavy Pressure
Vital energetic people possessing a strong character will usually write with heavier pressure than those of a more sensitive, timid disposition, thus more energy is being expended. (see Figure 29.) If heavy pressure is supported by positive traits in the writing, suggesting an outgoing, reliable personality, the writer

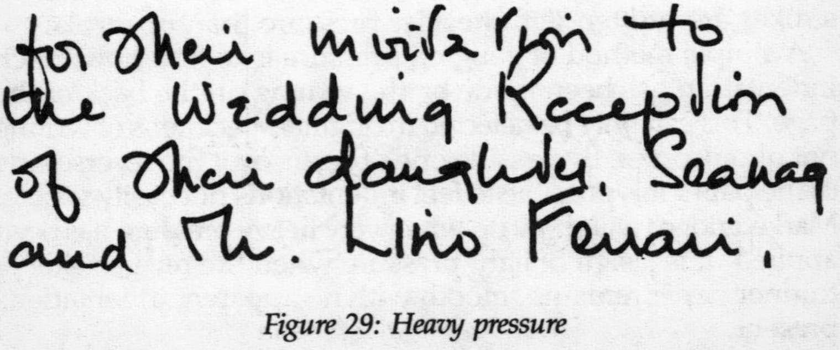

for their invitation to
the Wedding Reception
of their daughter, Seanag
and Mr. Lino Ferrari,

Figure 29: Heavy pressure

possesses the potential for great achievements. On the other hand heavy pressure can also be an indication of inner tensions building up without sufficient outlet, showing the presence of energy suppressed rather than being used to a profitable purpose. In this case heavy pressure will be accompanied by other negative features, the writing suggesting an inhibited, restricted disposition.

Light Pressure
In many cases (see Figure 30) light pressure signifies an agile, sensitive and adaptable mind. People of perception and those of a gentle disposition often write with light pressure. But on the negative side light pressure can indicate a weak person, showing little will-power or stamina. Other traits in the writing will help determine the correct interpretation.

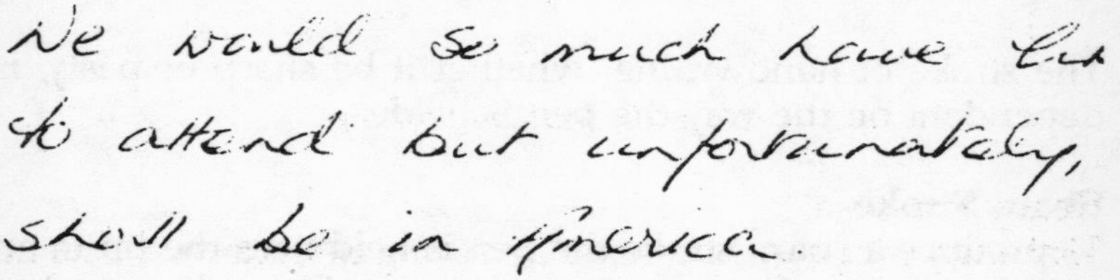

Figure 30: Light pressure

Irregular Pressure
Irregular pressure (see Figure 31) is best detected by turning the script upside down. The heavier strokes will then stand out

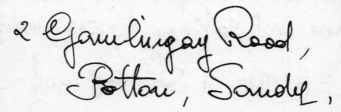

Figure 31: Irregular pressure

more distinctly. A regular pattern of pressure is sometimes interspaced by single strokes, letters, or whole words written with heavier pressure, suggesting a sudden onset of strong feelings which could be induced by the writer's own thoughts or the contents of the script. Such feelings of excitement, anger, irritation, or outbursts of energy often pass as quickly as they came and a regular pattern of pressure is resumed.

When there is a pattern of heavier pressure at the beginning of words it is a sign of pretentiousness, of the writer, maybe subconsciously, wanting attention. When heavier pressure is regularly applied at the end of words it is an indication that the writer likes to express authority, stubbornly emphasizing his or her own point of view.

Stroke

The stroke of handwriting, whether it be sharp or pasty, is dependent on the way the pen is held.

Sharp Stroke

To produce a sharp stroke the pen is held near the tip in an upright position. Sharp or fine writing (see Figure 32) often has light pressure, but under a magnifying glass it is possible to

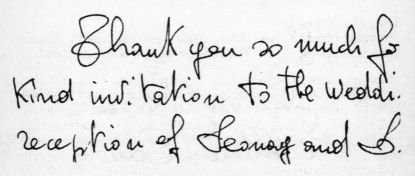

Figure 32: Sharp stroke

identify the difference between the up-strokes and down-strokes. Writers of a sharp script are usually well-disciplined. their interests mostly lie in the spiritual, intellectual and aesthetic fields. They tend to be sharp, accurate thinkers, best suited to work where accuracy, self-discipline, and critical assessments are required.

Pasty Stroke

Pasty writing (see Figure 33) has a thicker, heavier stroke produced by holding the pen like a paintbrush, higher up the stem and lying at an angle close to the paper. Pasty writing looks as though it has been painted, not written onto the paper, the heavy up and down-strokes showing little or no difference in appearance. Pasty writers tend to be less self-disciplined, more easy-going and sensual, their interests lying close to nature. Artists, farmers and gardeners will often show pastiness in their handwriting.

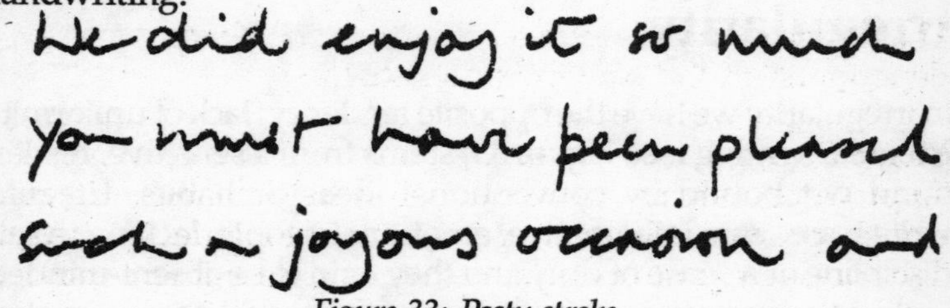

Figure 33: Pasty stroke

Regularity

A dictionary definition of 'regular' is 'uniform', 'constant', 'steady'. So in regular writing (see Figure 34), the height, width and slant of letters in the middle zone, the direction of lines and the strokes and loops are uniform. Writers of a regular script are generally self-disciplined, well able to keep their impulses and emotions in check. They are reliable and predictable, their actions usually being influenced by a strong sense of duty. But (depending on other traits in the writing), regularity can also be the indication of a dull personality possessing little original thought or excitability. In stiff writing (lacking rhythm), where regularity is seen to be rigid throughout the script, the writer could carry out a disciplined routine to the extreme, suggesting some degree of compulsive behaviour.

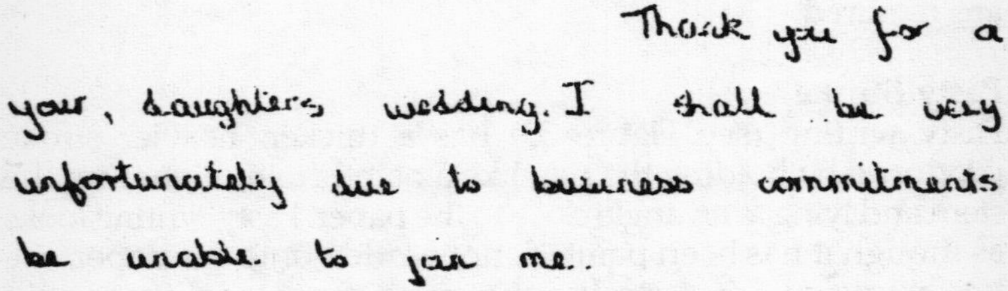

> Thank you for a your, daughter's wedding. I shall be very unfortunately due to business commitments be unable to join me.

Figure 34: Regular writing

Irregularity

In irregularity we have the opposite tendency; lack of uniformity. Irregular writing (see Figure 35) stems from a sensitive, restless mind not bound by conventional ideas or habits. Irregular writers are often imaginative, emotional people, lacking in self-discipline or a sense of duty and they tend to be absent-minded. Unlike the writers of a regular script they rebel against routine preferring to participate in variety and change, and are capable of working under chaotic conditions. Many talented creative

> If you would just provide a p not mind writing two or th

Figure 35: Irregular writing

people show irregularity in their writing. Some young people during adolescence when they are emotionally insecure and finding their feet in the adult world show irregularity in their writing. (See also Chapter 3, fluctuating slants.)

It stands to reason that untidy, badly proportioned writing need not necessarily be due to indolence or lack of initiative, as it may appear, but could be an indication of exceptional attributes or talents. For whereas well-balanced, reliable, predictable people, through their work, will usually show reasonably well-proportioned zones and a regular script, the writing of a person possessing an exceptional talent will tend to show an imbalance of zones, irregularity, and often signs of absent-mindedness such as missing i-dots or lack of punctuation, their energies and endeavours being channelled in one direction and mundane formalities being overlooked in the process.

Rhythm

Regularity and rhythm tend to go hand in hand for basically rhythm is an indication of the writer's sense of inner harmony. A rhythmic script flows forwards continually smoothly and easily suggesting emotional balance and stability. Unrhythmic script is when the flow of writing is disturbed by traits such as fluctuation in the size of the middle zone, an unsteady base line, and irregular spacing between letters and words producing a jerky appearance lacking in continuity of flow. Unrhythmic script suggests strong emotional changes with outbursts of temper, moodiness or excitability, in which case the handwriting may also show heavier pressure in some strokes and words. (See irregular pressure.)

Exercise 5

1 a How is pressure created?
  b How is pressure expressed?
  c What is the amount of pressure exerted proportional to?
  d What is the degree of pressure determined by?

2 In a regular pattern of writing which strokes are usually heavier and which lighter?

3 a List some characteristics of a writer of a uniformly heavy pressure when supported by positive traits in the writing.
  b What could be the implication of heavy pressure when accompanied by negative traits in the writing?
  c Suggest positive interpretations of light pressure.

4 Examine several samples of handwriting for degree of pressure. Is the pressure medium, light, heavy, or irregular with some strokes, letters or words written with heavier pressure? If the latter applies suggest reasons for the change in pressure.

5 a On what does the stroke of writing depend?
  b Name some characteristics of both sharp and pasty writers.

6 a Define regularity in handwriting.
  b Name some positive characteristics associated with regular writing.
  c What does irregularity signify? How do irregular writers differ from those of a regular script?

7 a What does the rhythm of writing indicate?
  b Describe the appearance of a rhythmic script.

8 a Describe the appearance of an unrhythmic script.
  b Suggest traits in the writing which could cause this appearance.
  c Name some characteristics of unrhythmic writers.

6. Right and Left Tendencies, Fullness/Leanness, Starting, End and Cover Strokes

Tendencies

As mentioned in Chapter 3 writing in the Western world starts on the left side of the page progressing across the sheet towards the right, the left becoming the writer's past, the position reached the present, and ahead lies the future towards which the writer is advancing. Whether this progress forwards is direct (to the right) or complicated by a pull to the past (to the left) is dependent on the writer's character.

Right Tendencies
Right tendencies (see Figure 36) are a progressive movement, features which speed up handwriting, assisting the forward flow of thoughts and actions by an increased pull to the right (towards the future and the outside world). Lean upper and lower lengths

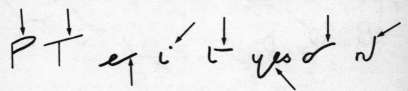

Figure 36: Right tendencies

count as right tendencies, so do drawn-out letters in the middle zone (wide secondary width), as time is not being lost in forming large loops or cramped-up letters which would deter forward movement.

Left Tendencies

Left tendencies (see Figure 37) are retrogressive features which impede the speed of writing and the natural inclination for self-expression and forward movement (towards the future and the outside world). The more left tendencies present in the handwriting the greater the influence of the past has on the writer.

Left tendencies introduce an element of caution. They can appear in the writing of people of sound common sense who stop to think, weighing a situation up carefully before making a decision. Egotists, the greedy, 'graspers' and 'hoarders' frequently show left tendencies in their writing. Sometimes a past experience (which could possibly have receded into the subconscious) will influence the use of left tendencies. The pull from the past attempts to restrain the writer's free flow of self-expression and forward movement.

Most writing will contain a few left tendencies. They act as a brake to over-hastiness, a restricting influence checking a head-long surge forwards without caution, which otherwise may spell disaster. But on the other hand too many left tendencies suggest emotional reticence, difficulty in forming relationships, lack of confidence and insufficient self-expression.

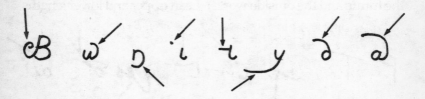

Figure 37: Left tendencies

Fullness and Leanness

Handwriting is described as 'full' when letter formation takes up more space than indicated by the copy-book form and 'lean' when writing occupies less space than the prescribed form (see Chapter 2). Full writing (see Figure 38) is attained by large loops, circles, flourishes and sweeping strokes, whereas lean writing (see Figure 39) is denoted by straight lines, narrow loops and angles rather than rounded formations.

Fullness shows imagination and often a creative mind, but can also indicate muddled thinking and a tendency to escape into a world of fantasy, but other features in the handwriting will be a guide as to the correct interpretation. Leanness indicates lack of imagination, lack of abstract thinking, but with the ability to deal with life's practicalities. It can also indicate a materialistic outlook and rigidity of thought.

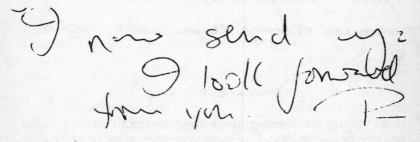

Figure 38: Full writing

Figure 39: Lean writing

Starting Strokes
Some people do not use starting strokes (see Figure 40). The first letter of a word is formed in the same way as they approach life — directly. They get straight down to a job, are not fussy, and are usually quickly able to differentiate between the essential and non-essential. Others need time to prepare for the task in hand, be it mental or physical. They have an inner need for preparation before action. These people show this characteristic in their writing by use of a starting stroke. They may, but not necessarily always, waste time and effort before action. There are various forms of starting strokes all of which serve the same purpose, but the expression is shown by the writer's own individual traits in his or her choice of starting stroke.

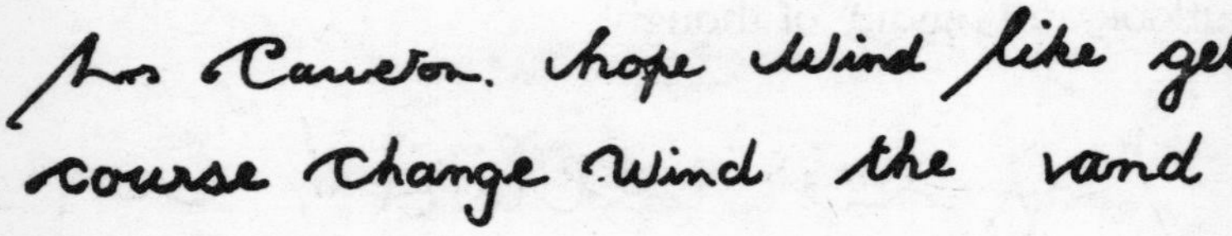

Figure 40: Starting strokes

A straight, stiff starting stroke suggests rigidity. a long stroke starting below the baseline is often an indication of aggressive or stubborn behaviour. A hook at the beginning or end of a stroke is another sign of aggression or self-assertion. It may also indicate tenacity, the writer wanting to hold on to something, not willing to let go. Starting strokes in garland formation denote a warm caring personality and generosity, whereas an arcade formation suggests a secretive nature. A very short stroke preceeding a word as in 'get' (Figure 40) is usually a sign of wanting to hold on to a familiar pattern of life.

End Strokes or Finals
Right and left tendencies can be seen in the end strokes of some

letters (see Figure 41), also for example the lyric 'd', 'w' and 'n' in Figure 37, the final strokes all pulling towards the left. Similarly strokes of letters such as 'T', 'e' and 'd' in Figure 36 show right tendencies, a pull to the right.

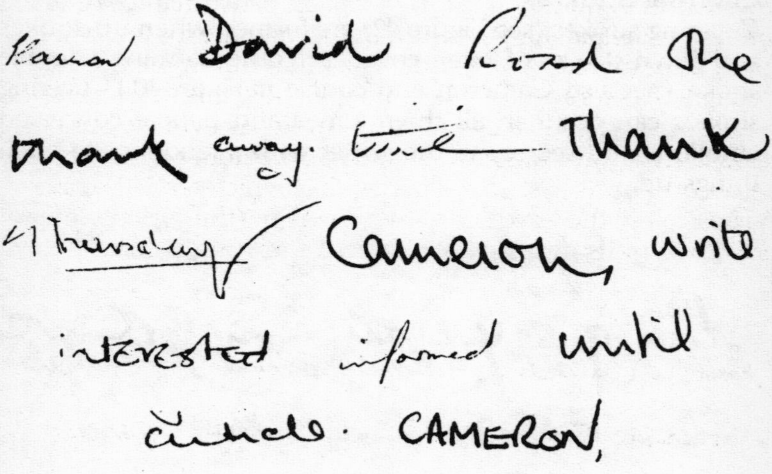

Figure 41: End strokes

A long drawn-out final stroke to the right suggests a 'worrier', someone who finds it difficult to let go of a problem, but may also indicate determination and haste to achieve the objective. The garland formation is again a sign of warmth or generosity. An end stroke as in the 'y' of Thursday in Figure 41 suggests high ideals of personal attainment. Finals dropping below the baseline are usually a sign of stubbornness, intolerance and a refusal to compromise. An end stroke turning back in a claw formation indicates a materialistic outlook, greed or emotional reticence and avoidance of responsibility. An end stroke extending straight upwards suggests enterprise, idealism or intellectual interests closely connected wth everyday life. When end strokes are short or missing the writer tends to show abrupt or terse behaviour. When there is a pattern of missing end strokes throughout the script this usually signifies a person prone to starting jobs but rarely finishing them on his or her own initiative.

Covering Strokes

Covering strokes (see Figure 42) are formed when up-strokes and down-strokes of letters cover each other forming a double stroke. (See also 'Cameron' and 'course' in Figure 40.) Covering strokes can occur in all three zones and denote concealed emotions and secrecy in the writer with a tendency to hush things up.

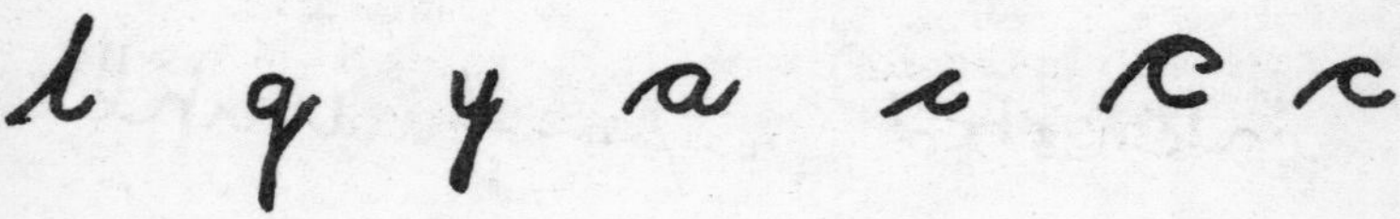

Figure 42: Covering strokes

Exercise 6

1 What are right tendencies?

2 Examine several samples of handwriting for right tendencies, such as lean upper and lower lengths, extended t-bars to the right, end strokes pulling to the right, i-dots to the right, loops of capitals extended to the right and drawn-out letters in the middle zone.

3 a What are left tendencies?

  b Name characteristics associated with the use of left tendencies.

4 Examine several samples of handwriting for left tendencies such as: end strokes turning to the left, extended underlengths pulling towards the left, inflated loops, i-dots and t-bars placed to the left.

5 a How is 'full' writing attained?

  b What does 'full' writing signify?

  c Describe 'lean' writing.

  d What does 'lean' writing signify?

6 a Why are starting strokes used?

  b What does lack of starting strokes suggest?

7 Examine several samples of handwriting for starting and end strokes. Note the type of starting strokes used (if any) and end strokes, and suggest characteristics associated with them.

8 a What are covering strokes, and what do they signify?

  b Examine samples of handwriting for covering strokes in all three zones.

7. Baseline, Spacing, Placement and Form Level

Baseline

The line on which the letters of a word are written is called the baseline, visible when lined paper is used or invisible and subject to the writer's personality when unlined paper is chosen. For the purpose of handwriting analysis the writer is asked to use unlined paper for otherwise the inclination to follow the ruled lines would deter the writer's natural expression of direction.

The direction of the baseline reveals the writer's feelings and emotions at the time of writing and can vary according to the mental and physical state of the writer, as well as the position in which the paper is placed when writing. Left-handed writers may need to adjust this position in order to gain maximum comfort and conveninence. The following interpretations are therefore more significant when the direction of lines in a specimen of handwriting shows a regular pattern. Several samples of handwriting written by the same person at different times are sometimes requested by the graphologist when an in-depth character analysis is required. Everyone has days of happiness and elation, and likewise fits of the blues or tiredness when nothing seems to go right, and the effects of these moods are reflected in their handwriting.

Straight Baseline

When the sheet of paper is placed in a straight position in front of the writer and the baseline is seen to be straight and regular (see Figure 43), a well-balanced, steadfast personality is indicated, one who is reliable, with good self-control and a sense of direction.

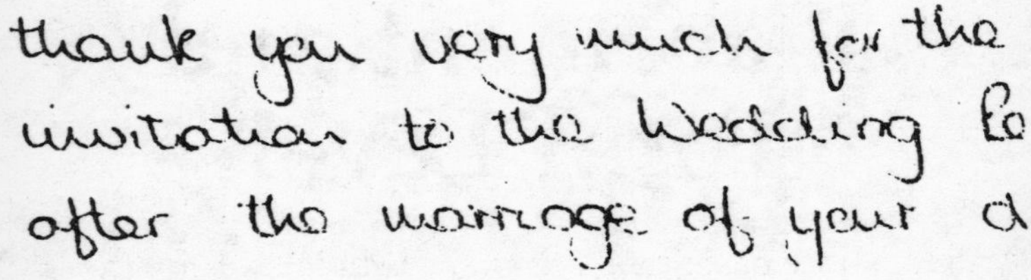

Figure 43: Straight baseline

Descending Lines

A regular pattern of descending lines (see Figure 44) suggests mental or physical fatigue, despondency, depression, or pessimism; conditions all of which may be of a temporary nature due to ill-health. Lines descending in a step-formation show the writer is fighting against these conditions.

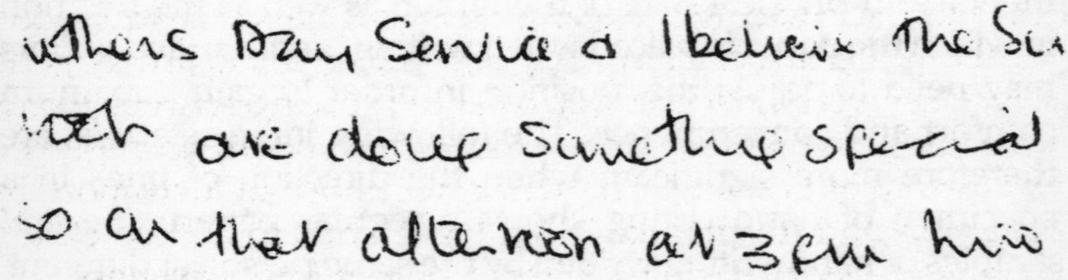

Figure 44: Descending lines

Ascending Lines

A script with regularly ascending lines (see Figure 45) signifies an excitable, enthusiastic, impulsive nature. An attempt to curb impulses is shown by the lines ascending in step-formation.

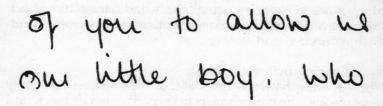

Figure 45: Ascending lines

Writers whose baseline continually undulates throughout the script tend to be unreliable, unstable, with feelings of insecurity and they have difficulty in making decisions. Convex lines indicate a fluctuation between bouts of enthusiasm and waning interest, whereas concave lines suggest the writer, after an enthusiastic start, will need to overcome doubts and fears before being bold enough to proceed.

Spacing Between Words and Lines

As with all features in handwriting the spacing between words and lines are not accurately significant on their own but must be considered along with the assessments of all other traits in the writing. Spacing between words and lines is an indication of the writer's sociability, and organizing capability. A good organizer will show clear, well-balanced spacing between words and lines, neither too wide or too narrow, often accompanied by a straight baseline. The writing of those guided more by intuition and imagination than logic tends to be less clearly arranged. Poor spacing is often a sign of impulsiveness.

Wide Spacing Between Words

Spacing is termed generous when the distance between words is wide but not over-wide (see Figure 46 for wide spacing between words and lines). Generous spacing suggests generosity and a cultured background, but may also be a sign of emotional instability and time-wasting. Where over-wide spacing occurs generosity could be carried to the point of extravagence. Very wide spacing can also indicate isolation. Such writers have difficulty in making friends and may appear stand-offish, conceited and over critical.

Wide Spacing Between Lines
When spacing between lines is too wide actions are rarely spontaneous. The writer prefers to keep his or her distance, and is guided more by reason than feelings and emotions.

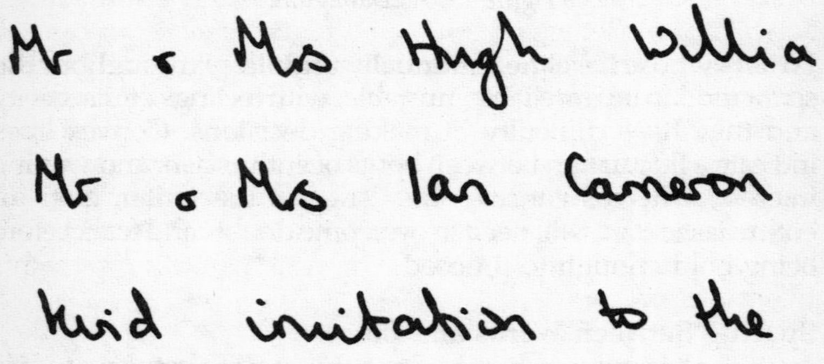

Figure 46: Wide spacing between words and lines

Narrow Spacing Between Words
Very narrow spacing between words (see Figure 47 for narrow spacing between words and lines) is indicative of prompt, impulsive actions, but spacing that is too crowded, with words touching or even overlapping, is a sign of muddled thinking

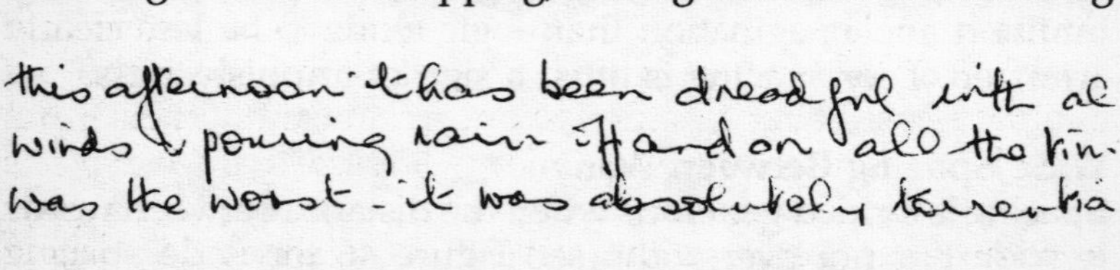

Figure 47: Narrow spacing between words and lines

and/or a great need to be in the company of others. Such people dislike being on their own and are at home in a crowd, but they lack objectivity.

Narrow Spacing Between Lines

Narrow yet distinct spacing between lines signifies a scrupulous, careful attitude. When spacing between lines and words is too narrow or appears to be muddled, with some words touching and upper and lower lengths mingling, emotional confusion is indicated. The writer is unable to think clearly or purposefully, is often weak-willed and tends to act on impulse.

When spacing is otherwise clear and distinct but the lower zones of some letters mingle with the upper zones of the line below there can be a close affinity between thinking and instinct; the writer's thoughts being influenced by feelings and instinct. Spacing between lines that grows narrower towards the bottom of the page can be a sign of a person who delays making a decision and taking action until the last possible moment, but other features in the writing such as thready connections, left slant and irregularity in the middle zone would support this interpretation.

Placement

When considering the placement of handwritten script a letter can be a good specimen to examine. The writer wishes to impart a message so he takes a fresh piece of paper, frequently unlined, on which to convey the communication. The message is the objective so becoming absorbed in the task, margin placement, direction of lines, spacing between words and letters and position of the signature (to be dealt with separately) are spontaneous, being a natural expression of the writer. If not brought to his notice the writer may not realize that the margins are small, wide, or non-existent and the signature placed to the extreme right, left or in the middle of the sheet. The whole motion has been carried out spontaneously. Most people form an established pattern in the presentation of their script, unless temporarily disturbed due to factors such as ill-health or over-excitement.

Margins

The size of margins indicates the writer's sense of economy (thrifty or generous) and whether he is holding onto the past or eager to meet the future.

Left Margin
The left margin represents the influence of the past. The absence of a left margin suggests reserve and a good sense of economy, a person prudent and careful in the management of private matters.

Narrow Left Margin
A narrow left margin shows a tendency to be thrifty. It can also indicate a preference for security and the known way of life. An initially narrow left margin, gradually widening, shows the writer who started out with caution is gaining confidence as he/she becomes involved in the message being expressed.

Wide Left Margin
A wide left margin indicates culture, a desire to get on with life, leaving the past behind and/or a preference for lavish living. Should the margin become narrower as writing proceeds down the page an underlying need for economy may be greater than the preference to live on a grand scale, showing an element of caution in the writer. An inconsistent left margin indicates confusion, inconsistency, indecision and a tendency to be moody.

Right Margin
The right margin represents the writer's approach to the future and the outside world.

Narrow Right Margin

A very narrow or lack of right margin suggests eagerness to meet the future without fear or reservation with a tendency to rush headlong into situations.

Wide Right Margin

A wide right margin shows fear of the future, reserve and an inclination to hold back rather than confront situations. Irregularity of the right margin suggests inconsistency, a fluctuation betwen surging forward and holding back, and also a spirit of adventure. A full page with no margins indicates a mixture of emotions, the need to hold onto the past, and the desire to face the future. It could also indicate an expansive personality who is lacking in tact and could invade another's privacy. Or it may be a sign of excessive economy bordering on meanness. Other features in the writing would be a guide as to the correct interpretation. Where the script is surrounded by wide margins, appearing like an island, the writer through feelings of fear and isolation has withdrawn from the outside world, pushing away the past and yet afraid to face the future. Consistently straight margins indicate a methodical and orderly mind and good management of finance.

Upper Margin

A wide upper margin could signify formality; a sign of deference for the addressee. A tradition adhered to in days when letter writing was taught as social etiquette, it may also be a sign of lack of confidence. A narrow upper margin represents a more direct approach, a lack of formality or economy.

Lower Margin

A wide lower margin suggests abruptness; a desire to end the communication. There are many reasons why the lower margin could be small or non-existent, such as the desire to use up all the available space, not knowing when to end the message, shortage of paper etc; some of which are of no great relevance to the graphologist.

Form Level

In estimating the form level of handwriting the overall presentation of the script is taken into consideration, the following features being examined:

Layout
Does the layout have a pleasing, tidy, harmonious appearance? Is the script well-placed? Are the margins consistent?

Spacing
Look carefully at the spacing between words and lines and the direction of the lines. Are the words well and evenly spaced? Is the direction of lines uniform? Is the spacing between lines consistent, too narrow, too wide or irregular? Is there any mingling between the upper and lower lengths?

Originality
Is the style of writing similar to that taught at school, or does the writing possess originality? If original has the writing retained its legibility?

Writing of high form level possesses originality, is legible, and has an overall neat appearance. The script is centrally placed with good even spacing between words and lines, the direction of lines uniform, with no mingling, and margins consistent. Such writers are of good intelligence, quick to differentiate between the essential and the non-essential, tend to think logically with good co-ordination between thoughts and actions.

There are degrees of form level varying from a low standard, average, and high as outlined. Assessing form level accuracy comes with practice and experience. It is a means of grading handwriting and is helpful when evaluating individual traits in the writing.

The higher the form level the more the interpretation of a feature tends to be positive. The lower the form level the more the evaluation tends to be negative. An average form level may have a positive or negative interpretation. Writers of an average form level are usually reasonably well educated with average ambitions and capabilities, whereas those of low standard have usually received little education and have no great desire to further their knowledge. Their writing tends to be slow with little originality. They go through life acting more on instinct than thought and reason. But form level does not depend on social or cultural background or educational standards. It is relevant to the writer's creative and intellectual capabilities and potential.

Exercise 7

1 a What is the name given to the line on which letters are written?
  b What do descending lines indicate and why do some lines descend in step-formation?
  c What do ascending lines indicate and why do some lines ascend in step-formation?
2 a Name some characteristics that could apply to a writer of continually undulating lines.
  b Give reasons for a pattern of convex lines.
  c Give reasons for a pattern of concave lines.
3 a What does spacing between words and lines signify?
  b What is poor spacing a sign of?
4 a What does wide spacing between words indicate?
  b What does wide spacing between lines indicate?
5 What is the significance of cramped, overlapping spacing between lines and words?
6 Examine several samples of handwriting for direction of lines and spacing between words and lines, noting your interpretations of these features.
7 a What does the size of the margins indicate?
  b What does a wide right margin indicate?
  c What does a lack of margins indicate?
8 Suggest interpretations for the size of the margins in several samples of handwriting.
9 Assess the form level of these specimens of writing after examining the layout, spacing, and originality as indicated in Chapter 7.

8. Letter Formation and Speed

Letter Formation

As we have seen from studying various characteristics in writing, such as size, width, slant, form and degree of connection, as well as examining specimens of handwriting for these features, individual handwriting can vary consideraby from the style taught at school. The shape of letters may remain similar to the copy-book form suggesting the writer behaves in a conventional manner, whether of good intelligence or otherwise. In most cases, however, there are some changes in letter formation influenced by the writer's individuality.

Simplification

When unessential parts of a letter are cut short (see Figure 48), but the letter still remains distinct and legible, writing is referred to as 'simplified'. So simplification, as its name implies, means simplified letter formation. Letters carrying a loop, such as l or y, with a straight stroke, i-dots and t-bars connected to the following letter, and direct connections from the middle and lower zones to the upper within words, are examples of simplification. Writers of simplified scripts are striving to reach the goal with the least possible hindrance. They are quick to recognize essentials and are able to make decisions unhampered by strong imagination, emotions or feelings. Simplification is often found in speed writing.

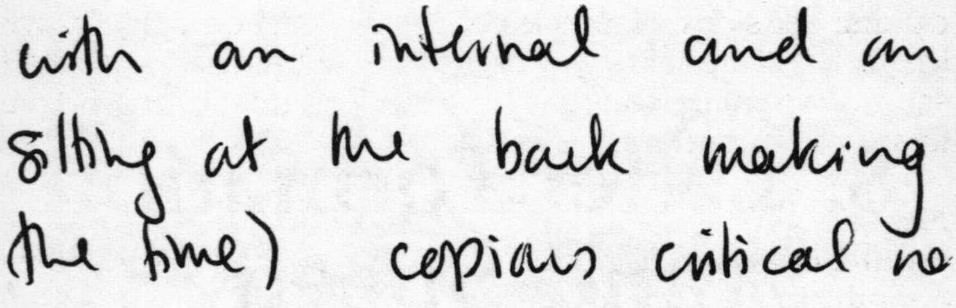

with an internal and an
sitting at the back making
the time) copious critical ne

Figure 48: Simplified writing

Flourishes

Flourishes (see Figure 49) are unnecessary sweeping strokes, loops, or curves which emphasize the unessential parts of a

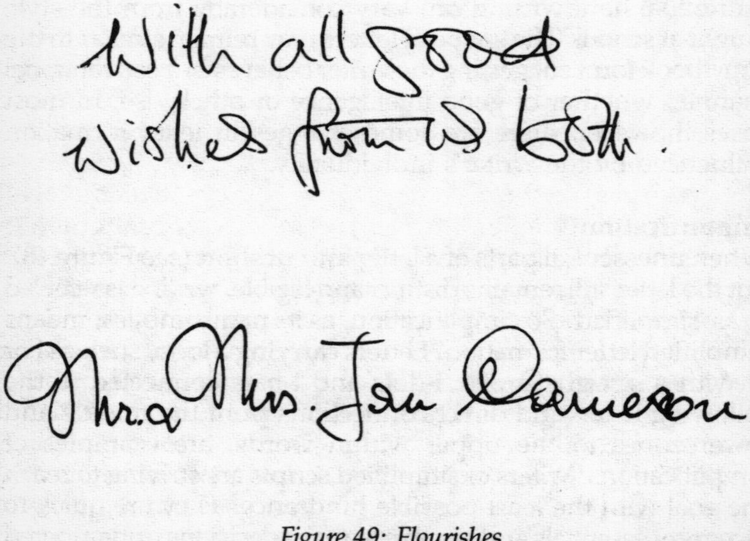

With all good
wishes from us both.

Mr. & Mrs. Ian Cameron

Figure 49: Flourishes

letter. They do not enhance the writing and may hinder legibility. Contrary to the writers of simplified script such writers tend to be over careful, lack clarity of thought and find difficulty in making decisions. Flourishes, therefore, can be a sign of playing for time, but are also a way of showing off, indicating a boastful self-important person, one who lacks originality and is trying to appear important.

Neglect

Writing is termed neglected when the essential parts of letters are indistinct or non-existent. Neglected writing can have several interpretations (see also Illegibility, Chapter 3). When the writing speed is slow neglect can be a sign of carelessness, laziness, and slovenly behaviour. In quick writing neglect may be due to the writer's thoughts flowing faster than they are able to be written down. Indistinct writing can also indicate the writer's wish, either consciously or sub-consciously, to remain inscrutable, which could, for example in the case of neurotics, be a fear of taking responsibility, or there may be some deeper reason for the wish to conceal or hush things up.

This course is not designed to give examples of all the various ways in which each letter of the alphabet may be written but to indicate the more general characteristics of letter formation as well as the special significance of the lower loops of g and y and the placement of i-dots and t-bars.

Certain aspects of letter formation have already been mentioned in Chapter 6 under the headings Right and Left Tendencies, Starting End and Cover Strokes. In Figure 50 other general characteristics of letter formation are illustrated.

Rounded formation is a sign of non-aggression and adaptability when letters are well-connected. Angular letter formation suggests a more aggressive, firm approach with less adaptability. other signs of aggression are hooks at the beginning and end of letters (see Chapter 6, Starting and End Strokes), angular lower lengths and angular connections between letters and zones. Very heavy pressure on down-strokes can also signify aggression.

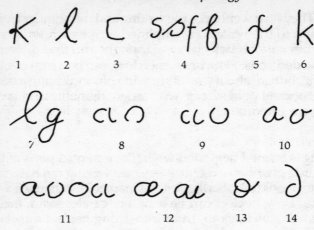

Figure 50: Letter formations

1 Knotted formation suggests tenacity, toughness and thoroughness, but may also show the writer's satisfaction in personal achievements when the loop is large.

2 Pointed tops to letters indicate an alert mind with a keen interest in everyday matters.

3 Square letters suggest creative ability possibly of a mechanical nature.

4 A variety of formations can indicate versatility, but may also point to unreliability.

5 A wavy line often indicates a sense of humour.

6 A stroke extended at the top suggests enterprise.

7 Large loops are a sign of imagination, but can also be a bid for attention.

8 A pattern of 'a's and 'o's open at the base indicates anti-social behaviour.

9 A pattern of 'a's and 'o's open at the top indicates openness, frankness or a talkative nature if the gap is fairly wide.

10 Closed 'a's and 'o's are a sign of secrecy, a person able to keep thoughts to themselves and respect the confidence of others.

11 A combination of both open and closed 'a's and 'o's shows

a good balance between frankness and secrecy indicating sincerity.

12 Two or more letters run together recurring in a script is another sign of secrecy.

13 A fortified 'o' suggests secrecy where facts are purposefully concealed and could signify insincerity, deceit, and scheming.

14 The lyric or Greek 'd' appearing frequently in the script can be a sign of literary interests or potential.

Single letters in the middle zone appearing inconsistently larger than other letters in the zone are a form of showing off, or wanting attention. The writer is most likely of an excitable disposition with a strong imagination. A pattern of the first letters of a word appearing larger than the rest is another bid for attention, but can also show that the writer is capable of taking the initiative, whereas the initial letters of a word regularly smaller indicates lack of initiative and may signify lack of confidence.

Lower Lengths of 'g' and 'y'

The way in which the underlengths of the letters g and y are formed (see Figure 51) give an indication of the writer's sexual and instinctive drives.

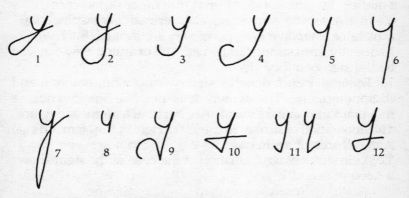

Figure 51: Lower lengths of 'g' and 'y' — 'y' illustrated

1 Underlengths pulled to the left show the writer is influenced by experiences in the past.

2 Large full underlengths are signs of strong imagination with instinctive and materialistic drives in money and sex, or a liking for the good things in life.

3 An open pull to the left is a sign of emotional immaturity and impressionability, often seen in the handwriting of young girls with a romantic outlook.

4 Exaggerated open rounded underlengths suggest a strong imagination whereby the writer may escape into a world of wishes, dreams and fantasy.

5 Simplified straight underlengths as mentioned under 'Simplification' indicate lack of fussiness, a quick grasp of situations with the ability to get down to essentials promptly, unhampered by imagination.

6 Long straight underlengths, as above with vitality, physical energy, and good organizing capabilities.

7 Long pointed thrusting underlengths are a sign of tension and could indicate a sharp tongue and critical attitude.

8 Very short or non-existent underlengths indicate stunted instinctive drives. In which case energies may be channelled into other spheres such as an all-absorbing business enterprise. But with emotions lacking a natural outlet frustrations could build up causing sudden bursts of temper or violence.

9 In the arcade formation, also termed a 'grasping claw', avoidance of emotional responsibility is indicated. Such writers frequently form strong family ties. The grasping claw can also be the sign of a 'hoarder'.

10 Triangular underlengths signify frustration, emotion and disappointment. The writer does not like interference, is intolerant and irritable, and may become a 'domestic tyrant'.

11 Small tick-like strokes to the left or right of the stem indicate some degree of aggression.

12 A closed concave formation at the base of the stem shows a need of security.

T Crossing

T-bars and i-dots are usually added after the letter has been written as a separate spontaneous movement. The bar of the letter 't' (see Figure 52) may be written with lighter pressure than that of the stem suggesting sensitivity, or heavier portraying energy and a strong will. A bar starting with light pressure becoming heavier indicates aggression, whereas heavier pressure becoming lighter suggest a very sharp wit or critical attitude. A rising bar signifies drive and enthusiasm and a falling bar despondency.

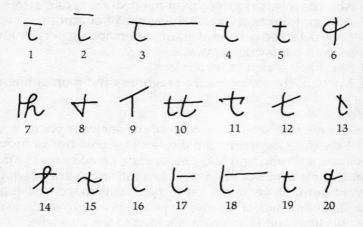

Figure 52: t-bar formations

1 Resting on top of the stem; bossy, ambitious wanting to be at the top.

2 High above the stem; high flying ideas, indulges in daydreams, unrealistic.

3 Protective, apt to patronize.

4 A sign of caution, delayed action.

5 Copy-book style, a balanced outlook.

6 A pride in own achievements or those of the family.

7 A form of simplification, a logical thinker with a quick grasp of situations, efficient.

8 Angular formation, determination, stubbornness, dislikes interference.

9 Ambition, aggression.

10 A quick grasp of situations with the ability to solve problems.

11 Hooks, persistence and stubbornness, mild aggression.

12 Enthusiasm, ambition and drive.

13 Falling bar, a sign of despondency but could also indicate weakness.

14 The looped stem can indicate vanity.

15 Wavy stroke; a sense of humour.

16 Absence of bar; a sign of absent-mindedness or carelessness.

17 A quick thinker, thoughts flying ahead of actions.

18 Long detached bar; enthusiasm, a demanding personality, ambition if bar swings upwards.

19 Short bar; a sign of repression.

20 Knotted; showing tenacity, toughness and thoroughness.

i-dots

The dot over the letter 'i' can be neatly or carelessly placed with light pressure suggesting timidity, average pressure, or heavy pressure, an indication of firmness, force or violence. The dot can assume a variety of shapes: as a full stop, circle, dash or accent form, an arc to the left or right, curved, convex, tent-like, or absent altogether, and be placed in a high, medium or low position and is sometimes joined to the next letter.

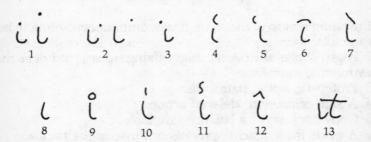

Figure 53: Placement and formation of i-dots

1 Overhead and near to the stem. Careful with attention to detail, methodical, with good powers of concentration. When the dot is high overhead a strong imagination is indicated with a not too realistic outlook.

2 Dot to the right. Enthusiasm with impulsive tendencies, haste. High to the right; imagination, enthusiasm, impulsiveness.

3 Dot to the left; caution, lack of spontaneity.

4 Arc to the right, often called the 'watching eye', observation.

5 The watching eye with left placement, observation, caution.

6 Convex formation; concealment of facts, deceit.

7 Dash formation; haste, often the sign of a lively personality.

8 Absence of dot. Carelessness, forgetfulness, can be a sign of the writer being absorbed in other matters.

9 In circle formation; call for attention sometimes found in the writing of young girls, creative ability with lack of direction.

10 Accent formation; criticism.

11 Wavy line; a sense of humour.

12 Tent formation; a sign of criticism.

13 Joined to the next letter; a form of simplification, speed, able to get down to essentials quickly, good judgement.

Speed

When assessing speed in handwriting analysis it is not necessary to know the number of words written or typed per minute as in shorthand and typewriting speeds, but it is important to ascertain which features are impeding or increasing the speed of the writing. Given below are examples of such features:

Slowing up Features	*Speeding up Features*
Left slant	Right slant
Left tendencies	Right tendencies
Descending lines	Ascending lines
Disconnected writing	Well-connected writing

Slowing up Features	*Speeding up Features*
Arcade and angular connections	Thread and garland connections
Flourishes, loops and curves	Simplification
i-dots to the left or placed overhead	i-dots to the right
Regular writing	Irregularity
Narrow writing	Wide writing
Heavy pressure	Light pressure
Short end strokes	Extended end srokes
Carefully formed letters	Carelessly formed letters

It will be seen from these lists that features tending to increase the speed of writing are those which enable the writer to take a direct route to the right, towards the future and the outside world, whereas slowing up features act as a brake to the writer's progress forward. A slow speed, therefore, suggests a cautious approach, which may be due to the presence of inhibitions which to some degree are holding back the writer's capacity for self-expression and communication with others. A fast speed, on the other hand, indicates the presence of relatively few inhibitions. In which case the writer's desire for self-expression and outgoing inclinations are comparatively unhindered.

Thus it follows that slower writing allows a greater degree of self-control. Thoughtful people who assess situations carefully before acting are often.slower writers. Also those who work steadily and reliably with no great desire for haste, the lazy, and some timid people tend to write at a slower speed.

Fast writing is often the indication of an alert, active mind, good adaptability and a quick grasp of situations, but may also indicate the type of person whose actions are carried out automatically with little insight or forethought and showing comparatively little individuality. People who regularly write at a great speed producing a hurried slapdash script tend, like the writers of an extreme degree of connection(see Chapter 4,

Extreme Degree of Connection), to be over zealous and often 'blind' to the feelings of others in their eagerness to achieve the objective.

Exercise 8

1 a What is meant by simplification?
  b Give three examples of simplification.
  c Name some characteristics associated with simplified writing.
2 a What are flourishes?
  b What does writing with a lot of flourishes signify?
3 Define neglect and suggest reasons for neglected writing.
4 Examine several samples of handwriting for simplification, flourishes and neglect.
5 a Specify signs of aggression in handwriting.
  b Give possible reasons for the following letter formations: square, letters formed in a variety of different ways, a wavy line, large loops, 'a's and 'o's open at the base, 'a's and 'o's open at the top, closed 'a's and 'o's.
6 a What do the underlengths of 'g' and 'y' indicate?
  b What do the formation of the following underlengths imply? Pulled to the left, stunted, large and full, as an arcade, triangular
7 Examine several samples of handwriting for letter formation noting whether the letters are formed similarly to the copy-book form or do they express the writer's individuality? How are the 'a's and 'o's formed? Are there a variety of letter formations? Are there signs of aggression, or does the writing have a rounded appearance? How are the underlengths of the 'g' and 'y' formed? Give interpretations of the size and shape of these underlengths.
8 While examining these samples of writing suggest characteristics associated with the placement and formation of the t-bars, likewise the i-dots referring to Figures 52 and 53 and corresponding interpretations.
9 How can the speed of handwriting be assessed and suggest reasons for fast and slower speeds?

9. Capitals, Personal Pronoun 'I', and Signature

Capital Letters

Capital letters are an indication of the writer's self-esteem and are often used to create an impression. When the size of capitals are in keeping with the main script they are termed 'average' and of no special significance. Capitals smaller in size suggest reserve, modesty, good powers of concentration and can also indicate lack of self-confidence, whereas the larger the capitals the greater the writer's self-regard. Very large capitals indicate ambition, pride or arrogance, and when also elaborated with loops or sweeping strokes pomposity or flamboyance. Narrow capitals can be a sign of shyness or a sense of economy depending on other features in the writing. Simplified capitals indicate straightforwardness and capitals formed in a different style from the main script imply versatility and independence. Capital letters standing apart from the following letter are a sign of intuition.

Personal Pronoun 'I'

The capital 'I' as a personal pronoun is an indication of the writer's ego, differing from the other capitals in that its formation expresses the writer's personal estimation of 'self'. If the capital I is in keeping with the rest of the script a healthy ego is indicated suggesting modest self-confidence. A straight simplified I is another sign of straightforwardness, with a good sense of judgement. Should the capital I be smaller, irrespective of the size of other capitals, the writer is expressing feelings of inferiority. A large capital I reveals feelings of superiority, and when inflated the writer is expressing considerable self-importance where in fact there is probably an underlying lack of confidence.

A capital I slanting to the left suggests withdrawl, anxiety or feelings of inferiority, but other features in the writing would confirm which interpretation is correct. Repression is expressed in the tall narrow formation and sentimentality or clinging to the past when the open base of the I swings to the left. When the capital I is regularly placed very close to the following letter leaving a gap to the left it shows the writer desires companionship and dislikes being or working alone. An I placed with a wider space on each side than shown between other words in the script is a sign of independence. If the I is regularly placed close to the preceding word lack of maturity is indicated. The writer is still holding on to the past. This trait is sometimes found in the handwriting of adolescents but disappears with growing confidence.

Signature

The signature is another ego symbol, but whereas the capital I as a personal pronoun expresses the writer's personal evaluation of self, the signature is usually an indication of how the writer would like to be thought of by others. When interpreting a signature the size, slant, form, and legibility should all be taken into consideration, and when possible assessed alongside the main script.

Each person's signature is unique. Some people have more than one signature, one used privately and one for business purposes. As our character develops so our signatures may change. One formed in early days can differ from the one used in later years, not only through maturity, but also due to our individual reactions to events that confront us throughout life. This fact has been observed when the signatures of some leaders and politicians have been examined over a period of years.

Christian names or initials are representative of the writer's private life, the surname the social side. When both Christian and surnames are similar in size, slant, and formation the writer's private and social lives are in harmony. If the letters of the Christian name are larger and more showy than those of the surname the private life is of prior importance. Should the Christian name appear smaller and poorly written compared with the surname the private life is of secondary importance to social activities. A difference in slant between the Christian and surnames indicates conflict between the writer's private and social obligations.

The writing of the main script is the true representation of character. When the signature is of the same size and identifies with the main script the writer is expressing a balance between private and public life with no desire to appear in public other than as the natural self. If the signature is smaller the writer, for some reason or other, wishes to appear of a more retiring disposition. A larger or more elaborate signature indicates a need to impress others. The greater the embellishments the stronger the need, which is possibly due to an underlying lack of self-confidence so the writer wishes to appear of considerable importance.

A difference in slant between the main script and signature shows the desire to create a false impression. For example, an upright script with a right-slanted signature is outwardly displaying a warm, friendly outgoing personality, where in fact the writer is naturally of a reserved independent disposition. A legible signature signifies straightforwardness with no desire to conceal identity, whereas an illegible signature may be due to the name being written so often it has developed into a scribble, or because the writer, for personal reasons, wishes to remain an unknown quantity.

Placement of Signature

These days, for business purposes, the signature is mostly placed under the typescript to the far left of the sheet, but when the placement is spontaneous, as in most handwritten scripts, the position is more dependent on the writer's personality. The extreme right position often accompanied by a general right placement of the script suggests enthusiasm, impatience and hastiness. A left placement shows a more retiring personality. Where there is an extreme left placement of the signature and script, withdrawl, anxiety and a sense of isolation are indicated. A central position suggests a cautious approach and need for security, and the normal position, a little to the right of the centre, suggests 'normality' in most things.

The writer underlining a signature is stressing self-importance. The line may be simple of light or heavy pressure or in the form of flourishes dependent on the writer's needs and could be acting as compensation for feelings of inferiority. An end stroke or separate line encircling the whole signature is a sign of anxiety, and in a similar way to the script being surrounded by wide margins (see Chapter 7, Wide Right Margin) the writer is creating a hiding place from the outside world. The signifance of a full stop after the signature is dependent on other features in the script, but can be the sign of caution, accuracy or an indication that the communication is now terminated.

Exercise 9

1 Give possible interpretations for small and very large embellished capital letters, and simplified formations.

2 What does the size and formation of the capital 'I' as a personal pronoun express?

3 What do the following formations of the personal pronoun 'I' signify?

    a An 'I' in keeping with the main script.

    b Smaller in size than the main script.

    c A large inflated 'I'.

    d A tall narrow 'I'.

4 What does a signature indicate, and what factors can influence a change in signatures during a person's lifetime?

5 a What do the Christian names or initials and the surname of the signature indicate?

    b Give possible reasons for a larger and more pronounced Christian name, a larger surname with a smaller Christian name, and the Christian names and surname slanting in different directions.

6 a Which writing is the true representation of character should they differ in size and/or slant, the main script or the signature?

    b Give possible reasons for: a signature smaller in size than the main script, larger than the main script, and the signature slanting in a different direction.

7 Suggest reasons for:

    a Legible and illegible signatures.

    b Extreme right and left placements of the signature.

    c Underlined and encircled signatures.

8 Examining several samples of handwriting, preferably letters, suggest interpretations for the size and formation of capital letters, 'I' as a personal pronoun, and signatures.

10. Addressing an Envelope

A dictionary definition of envelop is: 'to cover by wrapping, to surround entirely, to hide' and an envelope described as: 'that which envelops, wraps or covers'.

As mentioned in Chapter 3 writing is a means of communicating with other people and, when legible, is easily and correctly read. As time and trouble have been taken preparing the message in the envelope, the reason then for writing the address is that it will reach its destination without difficulty. In which case the writing on the envelope should be well arranged, clear and legible. This is achieved by many people, some writing more legibly on the envelope than in the letter itself, others printing the address, making an extra effort for the letter's safe arrival.

But for some people this appears an impossibility, for although they too wish the addressee to receive their communication, for why else would it be sent, their writing is illegible and numbering indistinct. See Figure 54.

When this happens time is then wasted by others attempting to determine the correct address, or in returning the letter should the sender's own address be legible, thus showing lack of consideration for other people.

The writing on an envelope does not necessarily reveal character in the same way as an analysis of the contents of the

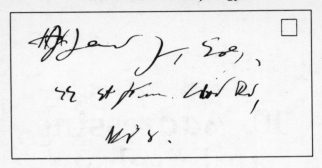

Figure 54

letter itself, but in comparison may bring to light other important traits in the writer's character hitherto not known.

Such cases of illegibility as shown in Figure 54 can signify that the writer has problems in consideration for other people and making his or her meaning clear, and may have difficulty in seeing the other point of view or expressing the meaning diplomatically.

The manner in which an envelope is addressed expresses the attitude of the writer to the outside world, how he or she behaves outwardly and would like to appear and be thought of by other people. The writing is particularly revealing when differing from that in the letter, for it then shows the true self and the appearance displayed are not in harmony. Figure 55 is an example of the writing of a considerate, genuine, unpretentious person who does not attempt to be anything other than he or she is. The writing is legible, clearly spaced and was not at variance with that in the letter.

In Figure 56 the writing on the envelope was found to be smaller and more confined than in the letter, which was larger, wider and more relaxed. It would appear from this comparison that such a writer has more self-confidence and ability than is apparent, but lacks self-assertion in social life.

The opposite type of personality is illustrated in Figure 57 where the envelope is addressed with heavier pressure and

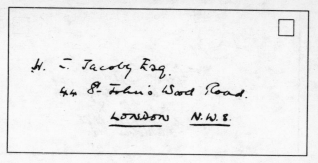

Figure 55

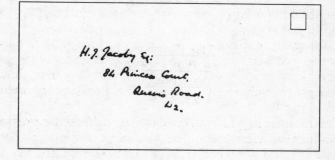

Figure 56

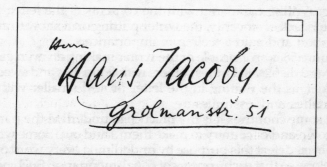

Figure 57

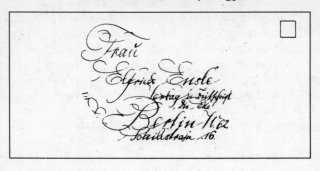

Figure 58

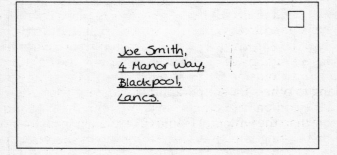

Figure 59

larger writing compared with the contents of the letter. Here there is lack of sincerity, the writer putting on a show to attract attention and gain a feeling of importance.

Figure 58 is an example of the writer making an even greater outward display to impress others with flourishes and sweeping strokes, as the writing in the letter proved smaller with few flourishes and less pressure.

In some countries it is the practice to underline the name of the town and/or country to make them stand out. Some writers, however, defeat this purpose by underlining every word on the envelope so that each appears of equal importance. Such people can experience difficulty in recognizing the difference between important and unimportant things in their lives. See Figure 59.

Besides the degree of legibility and variance between the writing of the address and the letter itself the spatial arrangement of the address is also significant and is found to be fairly consistent for each individual. In Figure 54 an example of the address centrally placed, clearly spaced and legible has already been illustrated.

Some people place the address to the left-hand side of the envelope as in Figure 60. Earlier in the course it was mentioned that left of a perpendicular drawn to the baseline and tendencies to the left signify influence of the past and the writer's ego. Using this interpretation for left placement of the address such writers are clinging to the past, wary of the future and may appear self-sufficient and reserved, not readily able to make new friends.

When the address is placed to the far right-hand side of the envelope as shown in Figure 61 the opposite interpretation applies for right placement and tendencies to the right express a pull to the outside world and the future. These writers are looking to others for support and friendship. They enjoy and need the company of others, escaping from the past and less capable than the writers of Figure 60 of managing on their own.

If the writing is placed to the very top of the envelope as in Figure 62 the writer is showing detachment from reality and the desire to escape into a dream world, an interpretation similar to that of t-crossings set high above the stem.

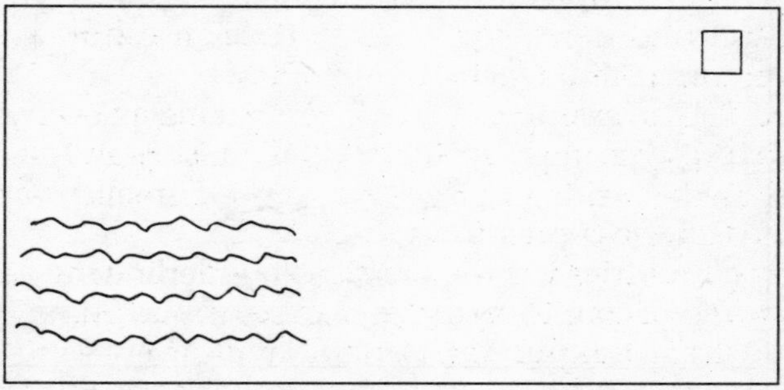

Figure 60

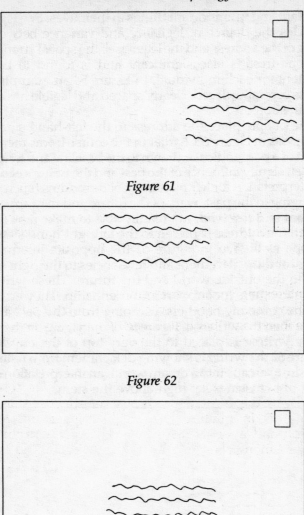

Figure 61

Figure 62

Figure 63

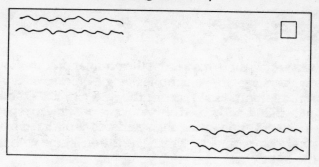

Figure 64

Figure 63 shows the address placed to the base of the envelope. Here the writer is expressing an over dependence on material things, easily depressed when confused with practical difficulties. The writing may also show descending lines.

An interesting spatial arrangement is shown in Figure 64, where the address is split up between the top left-hand corner and the lower right-hand side leaving an empty space in the middle. Referring back to the significance of the 3 zones, the upper zone represents the spiritual and intellectual attitude, the middle zone the emotional sphere, our likes and dislikes and approach to everyday life while the lower zone lays emphasis on the material, practical and instinctive side of life. Bearing this in mind such spatial arrangements suggest outwardly and in social relationships the writer lacks emotional response although is able to deal with intellectual and material matters.

Figures 54-58 inclusive are taken from *Analysis of Handwriting* by H. J. Jacoby: George Allen & Unwin Ltd, London, 1939.

Exercise 10

Letter writing these days is not the popular pastime it was many years ago, the telephone being a quicker means of communication. However, for the next exercise examine as many hand-addressed envelopes as possible for spatial arrangement and writing characteristics as outlined in the chapter, comparing the writing on the envelope with that in the letter.

11. Analysing Handwriting

Analysing handwriting is both a science and an art. The science lies in correctly interpreting features of the writing, and as many specimens of handwriting show contradictory characteristics the art is correlating these findings into an accurate character 'portrait' of the writer, which takes time. The obvious features, for example: size, slant, form and degree of connection show the more easily recognized characteristics of the writer such as whether he or she is modest or ostentatious, independent or needing company, warm-hearted and generous or formal and thrifty. But the individual stroke and letter formations reveal underlying, less apparent characteristics.

There are both positive and negative interpretations for all features in handwriting. The form level (see Chapter 7) gives an indication as to which interpretation. The higher the form level the more features tend to be positive. The lower the form level the more evaluation tends to be negative. In analysis a quality of the writer should not be stressed unless there are three or more substantiating factors. Both age and sex of the writer should be revealed in advance (see Introduction) and preferably the specimen written on unlined paper.

Taking a fresh sheet of paper as your worksheet first gain an overall impression of the writing then estimate the speed and form level as outlined in Chapters 8 and 7 respectively. The

96 *An Introduction to Graphology*

assessment of form level will give a guide as to the positive or negative interpretation of other features in the writing.

On your worksheet, under separate headings, make notes of your observations for each aspect of the writing as listed below, and possible interpretations, referring where applicable to the appropriate chapter.

Feature of Writing	Chapter
Speed	8
Form Level	7
General Impression of Writing	
Regularity (of m/z)	5
Slant	3
Rhythm	5
Horizontal Tension (driving force) *See example* *Specimen 1*	
Pressure	5
Absolute Size	2
Relative Size (the 3 zones)	1
General Layout (placement — margins)	7
Direction of Lines	7
Spacing between Words	7
Spacing between Lines	7
Width (of m/z)	2
Secondary Width (width between letters)	2
Degree of Attention (desire to impress others such as: flourishes, exaggerated capitals, superfluous strokes, larger initial letter, flamboyant signature or one larger than script)	
Formation of Letters	8
Character and Description of Stroke	5
Amendments	
Legibility	3
Starting Strokes	6
End Strokes	6
Degree of Connection	4
Form of Connection	4

Feature of Writing	**Chapter**
Fullness/Leanness	6
Covering Strokes	6
Right/Left Tendencies	6
i-dots	8
t-bars	8
Signature	9
Capital 'I' as Personal Pronoun	9

After reading through the interpretations for each individual feature draw up a quality–evidence sheet indicating the salient qualities of the writer and evidence found to support them.

The 'Portrait'

As some interpretations may appear contradictory, for example there could be signs of lack of confidence and insufficiency in what otherwise appears an outgoing personality with plenty of drive, the skill now lies in correlating all the traits to form an overall character 'portrait' of the writer. This becomes easier with practice.

A full analysis of the handwriting of Specimen 1, a male aged 65 years, is given overleaf as an example to study. (Note: sample has been reduced in size.)

1 I am afraid that John does not
2 have a very reliable estimate of the size
3 of the market he is intending to supply.
4 He has not identified his competitors, let
5 alone their probable strength.

6   Because he does not know the size
7 of the market he has no precise idea of
8 the amount of stock-in-hand he will
9 require to carry. If he carries too little
10 he will create a bad impression on
11 his customers. If he carries too much, he
12 will be locking up capital which could
13 otherwise be earning.

Sample 1

Full Analysis of Specimen No. 1 Male Age 65 Years

Work Sheet

Speed
By examining the writing for features which impede and increase speed as outlined in Chapter 8 the speed was assessed as being slightly slower than average.

Form Level
Form level (see Chapter 7) was estimated as being above average, indicating a tendency towards positive interpretations of individual traits in the writing, showing the writer to be of good intelligence and quickly able to differentiate between essentials and non-essentials: the slower speed expressing self-control and reserve. A thoughtful level-headed type of person who would stop to consider a situation before acting. The presence of inhibitions may also be slowing up the writing.

General Impression
Constrained writing with emotions and actions kept under control.

Regularity (of m/z)
m/z	height	slightly irregular with a few larger and smaller letters.
m/z	width	slightly irregular.
m/z	slant	irregular, mostly conflicting between upright and to the left, with a few letters slanting to right.
	lines	irregularly ascending in step-formation.

A rigid control over emotions and actions. Presence of inner conflicts shown by conflicting slant. A reserved disposition — the desire to drive forward restrained. Direction of lines expresses controlled ambition and enthusiasm. Does not readily conform to convention.

Writing Angle (slant)

u/z   conflicting between upright and slightly to the left.

m/z   mostly conflicting between upright and to the left with some letters slanting to the right.

l/z   upright or slightly to the left.

Shows inner conflicts between the desire for freedom of self-expression and reticence. Of an independent disposition the writer may experience feelings of loneliness at times, and behaviour fluctuates between reticence and some social excitability. The writer may experience difficulty in finding a firmly established purpose in life.

Rhythm

Appears stiff.

Horizontal Tension

(The driving force — impeded by roundabout movements, left tendencies, letters not reaching the baseline, fluctuation in slant and in width and size of letters i.e. all features which weaken the force driving towards the right.)

Varies — impeded by fluctuating slant, letters not reaching the baseline, breaks in connections between letters in words, some roundabout movements — showing a somewhat erratic drive forwards, but capable of an all out effort to reach the goal when interest is held. (See also degree of connection.)

Pressure

Furrows on the reverse side of the paper shown on the original specimen were easily felt by the fingertip, one indication of the overall strong pressure of the writing. Although some strokes, mostly covering strokes, are written with heavier pressure, the overall consistently strong pressure suggests materialism, energy and will-power. The strength of pressure in some t-bars points to the ability to persevere with plans, but the slower speed and strength of pressure suggests a build up of energy without sufficient outlet. The presence of some split pressure (pressure in side-strokes, up-strokes and down-strokes) could indicate some degree of aggressive feelings.

Absolute Size (size of the combined length of the 3 zones) 10-12mm dominantly 11mm.
Above average, but not over-large writing, showing a tendency for liking to do things on a grand scale.

Relative Size (size and combination of 3 zones)
u/z   height 1-4mm dominantly 4mm
m/z   height 1-2mm dominantly 2mm
l/z   height 4-8mm dominantly 5mm
Variance in height of individual zones — evidence of strain. Slight dominance of l/z showing material interests and a good foundation to the personality — feet firmly on the ground. Indicates good intellectual and/or spiritual aspirations. The small m/z in proportion to the full length suggests reticence in social relationships. A small m/z combined with careful punctuation and placement of i-dots, legibility and clear spacing is an indication of intellectual clarity, attention to detail, good powers of observation and the ability for sober-minded criticism. The imbalance in the small size of m/z compared with the full length brings feelings of restlessness — so projects may be started but not always finished before there is a desire to embark on a new interest. (See also horizontal tension.)

General Layout
Script well placed with top and lower margins balanced. Left margin straight, with left and right margins consistent suggesting methodical handling of financial affairs and good business sense. Constant in behaviour.

Direction of Lines
Irregularly ascending in step formation indicating enthusiasm, ambition and animation — kept in check. Not prone to acting on impulse.

Spacing Between Words
Well and clearly spaced, with fairly even distance between

words. There is a tendency for some words to be joined together. (See degree of connection.)

Spacing Between Lines
Clearly spaced — fairly wide in places e.g. between lines 3-4. Word and line spacing shows the desire to think things out clearly and to survey a situation before acting. (See also direction of lines.) It also indicates good organizing capabilities. The fairly wide spacing between lines suggests a feeling of standing apart from others, being somewhat of a loner.

Width (width between downstrokes in m/z compared with their height)
A little irregular tending towards being slightly narrow combined with the strong pressure indicating a controlled, reserved disposition — hiding emotions and feelings, also indicating good powers of concentration and observation but not a great deal of imagination. Good planning capabilities, but the degree of width with an upright and slight left slant shows caution.

Width Between Letters (secondary width)
Medium — wide, wider as in: line 6 'because', line 8 'amount', line 10 'bad', line 11 'much'. This show of width between letters is in contradiction to the restrictive influences also observed in the script, showing a generous side of the writer's personality, one that is willing to oblige and help others and has a liking for good living.

Degree of Attention (desire to impress others)
Slightly larger capitals in the script, but it is most noticeable in the size of the signature and the slant of the capital 'I' in the signature compared with the script.

Formation of Letters
Some letters that are open to the right, as in line 4 'competitors' and line 10 'he', give evidence of pressure from the future and the ability to face up to problems with fighting spirit. The

letter formation is somewhat rigid with conflicting slants. Some sharpening of t-bars (see t-bars) and loops indicate underlying feelings of aggression or self-assertion. Upper strokes of 'p' extending upwards, as in line 10 'impression', is an indication of enterprise. The simplification of some letter formations shows intelligence and realism. Some end strokes dropping below the baseline, e.g. line 2 'reliable', is a sign of obstinacy, firm convictions and self-assertion. Loops in l/z set at the base of the stem, as in line 2 'very' and line 13 'earning', is another sign of a loner. Counter strokes (the stroke forming a counter movement) as in line 1 'afraid' suggest opposition to conventional behaviour. Enrolment as seen in line 2 'have' and line 7 'idea' indicate secrecy (also indicated in covering strokes). The end letters tend to decrease in size showing intelligence. Some 'a's and 'o's are open, some are closed and these can indicate sincerity. An angular top to connections as in lower lengths of some 'f's, as in line 7 'of', shows a dislike of interference in affairs.

Character and Description of Stroke

The strokes are rigid with some shaky and weak strokes, see line 12 'which', some letters are neglected, see line 13 'otherwise', showing signs of inner conflicts and strain. Strokes are pasty, note some ink-filled loops, and this person enjoys 'creature comforts'.

Amendments

One amendment has been made with heavy pressure, see line 5 'probable'. The original letter was written twice, so it would appear concentration was disturbed.

Legibility

All words are legible but a few letters are not. The overall script is legible showing consideration for others combined with good layout showing clarity of thought.

Starting Strokes

There is occasional use of small starting strokes such as in line 1 '*t*hat' and line 3 '*i*ntending' indicating some need for inner preparations before starting a job.

End Strokes

There are several end strokes, e.g. line 2 'reliabl*e*', line 5 'alon*e*', which drop below the baseline. This is an indication of obstinacy, firm beliefs and of seldom thinking that the opinion of others is right. There is also a tendency to be dogmatic. Finals ending abruptly suggests a certain abruptness in the writer, including the ability to end relationships abruptly.

Degree of Connection

Overall the writing shows a slightly below medium degree of connection with the letters of most small words connected together and in larger words breaks in connection between 3-6 letters. The writer thus shows a medium degree of adaptability in mind and behaviour, good powers of reasoning and observation, intuition and can at times be irritable and tense. In line 3 the words 'of the' are joined together, and in line 4 'not identified' and line 7 'of the' also appear to be connected, but on further examination a slight break in connection between the words can be seen. This tendency to join words together shows the ability to become so absorbed in a project that, at the time, one becomes unaware of what is going on around oneself, and difficult to influence.

Form of Connection

Mainly arcade with a few angles and angular connections between zones, showing reserve, diplomacy, caution, secrecy, firmness and loyalty with a tendency to be formal in behaviour.

Fullness/Leanness (coverage of space)

u/z   lean
m/z   lean with occasional full letters e.g. line 1 '*does*', line 4 '*identified*', line 12 '*locking*', with some wide spacing between letters.

l/z   dominantely lean with some fuller loops.
The coverage of space points to rational thinking with a good
business sense and a creative imagination in material matters,
clear-sightedness and a critical sense but underlying warmth,
although emotions are not easily shown.

Covering Strokes
Covering strokes are present in all zones showing intellectual
independence, secretiveness and difficulty in freedom of
expression thus giving an outward show of formal behaviour
covering emotions and depth of feeling. Covering strokes also
suggest the presence of inhibitions.

Right Tendencies
u/z   t-bars extending to the right, lean u/z some i-dots to
         right.
m/z   some wide spacing between letters.
l/z   some lean lower lengths.

Left Tendencies
u/z   line 3 'of' connection of 'o' to 'f' pulled to the left, looped
         stems of 't'.
m/z   some letters e.g. 'o' in 'does' line 1 movement to the left,
         enrolment in some formations e.g. 'a' in 'have' line 2.
l/z   lower length of 'f' in 'of' line 7, some larger loops to the
         left.
Direct thinking, moving rationally towards one's goal with little
interference. Left tendencies in m/z suggest restrictive influences
holding the writer back from self-expression. The type of loops
in l/z suggest a 'loner' while the occasional fullness suggests
a strong tendency for material matters.

i-dots
Mainly the i-dots are placed over the stem showing accuracy
and attention to detail, and the fairly high placement of some
idealism. The dash formation of several of them suggests that

a lively interest is being taken in the subject in hand, while those in arc formation, such as line 12 'locking' and line 13 'otherwise', (watching eyes) shows good powers of observation.

t-bars

Mostly they are of good pressure indicating firmness and will-power. Those extending from the top of the stem over other letters, e.g. line 1 '*that*', line 2 '*the*', shows ambition, authority, and a sense of protection. The two bars set to the left, in line 4 '*not*' and line 6 '*not*', indicate caution and procrastination. Underlying aggressive tendencies are suggested in bars sharpening at the end, e.g. line 9 '*too*', which also has a small hook at the start. Bars in convex formation as in line 4 '*competitors*' are another indication of self-control. The varied formation of t-bars point to a man of many wills.

Signature

The capitals in the signature are larger than those in the script with the 'I' of a different formation slanting to the right while the capital 'C' is upright. The small letters in the signature are of similar size and form to those in the script with the 'm' in angular formation and the last two letters as threads extend in a line to the left, which, with a sharp angle, extends further to the right with heavier pressure. The extra large 'I' is written in a different form from that of the script and is slanting to the right, whereas the writing in the script fluctuates between upright and to the left, suggesting the writer would like to appear a more outgoing and important personality rather than the independent and more reticent 'self'. The difference in slant between the initial of the first name and the 'C' of the surname could indicate some conflict between the writer's private and social life, the private being of prior importance. This difference in slant could also be due to some restrictions in freedom of expression in the past and the desire (subconsciously) to rebel against it. The extended end stroke to the left then the right appears to be a forceful act of emphasis. The placement of signature to the right is a display of action and some impatience, the heavier pressure in the 'I' gives energy and emphasis and the rising surname gives ambition and enthusiasm.

Capital 'I' as Personal Pronoun

The 'I' as a personal pronoun is larger than the letters 'I' in the script and set further away from 'am' than the distance between most words, it also tilts slightly to the left and the down-stroke is written with less pressure than most other down-strokes. These observations suggest that the writer is considerably self-conscious and although he has a good opinion of himself there are underlying uncertainties and conflicts. The formation of the capital 'I' as a personal pronoun and others in the script suggests culture and a business-like approach to life.

Quality	Evidence
Good intelligence:	Above average form level, simplification, tendency for the letters to decrease in size towards the end of words, small m/z.
A rational thinker, clear-sighted, readily able to distinguish essentials from non-essentials; a realist able to give sober-minded criticism:	Above average form level; overall slightly lean writing, small m/z compared to full length combined with careful punctuation and placement of i-dots over the stem; simplification, good spacing and layout.
Level-headed, surveys and considers a situation before acting. A good planner, pays attention to detail, and has good powers of concentration and observation:	Good spacing between lines and words, strong pressure with slower speed, firm t-bars, some long, i-dots over the stem, narrowed width of m/z, small m/z in proportion to full length, 'watching eyes'.

Quality	Evidence
Materialistic, a good organizer, good business sense and an ability to handle financial affairs:	Straight left margin, margins consistent, l/z dominant, good layout, good spacing between lines and words.
Does not willingly conform to convention showing intellectual independence, a strong authoritive personality, and is difficult to influence with underlying aggressive and obstinate tendencies:	Irregularity of m/z, some counter strokes and movements, covering strokes in u/z, strong pressure, firm t-bars, some t-bars and loops sharpening , some split pressure, hooks, a tendency for some words to be joined together, some angular connections, end strokes dropping below the baseline, t-bars extended over other letters.
Behaviour fairly consistent:	Good layout and consistent margins.
Medium degree of adaptability:	A medium degree of connection (or slightly below), some angular and some rounded formation of letters.
Signs of secrecy:	Covering strokes in all zones, arcade formations, enrolment in 'o', 'a' and 'd' formations.
Ability to overcome difficulties:	Firm t-bars, strong pressure, upright writing with some left slant, some letters open to the right, angular connections. See strong personality.
Underlying warmth, generosity showing consideration and a willingness to help and protect others:	Some wide spacing between the letters in m/z, legible writing, t-bars extending over other letters.

Quality	Evidence
Desire to impress others:	Mainly seen in the signature, (no superfluous strokes, flourishes or over-large capitals).
Shows some inner need of preparations before starting a job:	Presence of small starting strokes.
If necessary this person is able to end relationships abruptly:	Finals ending abruptly.
Holds a good opinion of himself:	Capitals of a good size, Capital 'I' as a personal pronoun is a good size.
Rarely acts on impulse, shows self-control over actions and emotions:	Covering strokes, slower speed, t-bars are convex, lines ascend in step-formation, slightly irregular and fairly narrow m/z, slants are upright and to the left, leanness, rigidity of letter formation, i-dots and t-bars inserted, and some angular connections.
The person is reserved and independent tending to be formal in behaviour but with an underlying desire to appear more outgoing:	Upright and slants to the left, slants conflict in m/z, m/z small compared to the full length, difference in slant and the size of capital 'I' in the signature with that of the script and larger 'C' in signature; arcade connections.
Signs of strain and restrictive influences:	Constrained writing, weak strokes, some neglected letters, a slight tilt to the left of 'I' as a personal pronoun, difference in the size and slant of 'I' in the

Quality	Evidence
	signature and script, conflicting slants in m/z, slower than average speed, left tendencies in m/z, variance in the height of the zones, small m/z in proportion to full length.
Feelings of loneliness at times, signs of a loner:	Type of some loop formations in l/z, conflicting slants to the left and upright, capital 'I' as a personal pronoun set a little apart, fairly wide spacing between the lines.
Signs of caution and procrastination:	Some t-bars to the left, slightly narrow writing with upright and slant to the left, some initial capitals and letters standing away from the next letter, speed slower than average.
Uneven driving force, restlessness, tendency to change interests, may have difficulty in finding an established purpose:	Small size of m/z compared to full length, fluctuating slants, weakened horizontal tension.
Ambitious and enthusiastic:	Ascending lines and signature, firm long t-bars.
Enjoys creature comforts:	Pasty writing, some ink-filled loops, above average absolute size of writing, width between the letters wide in places.

'Portrait'

Outwardly the writer appears formal and reserved keeping his feelings and emotions well under control. He is level-headed and rarely acts on impulse, tending to survey and consider a situation before making a decision. A planner with good powers of observation and concentration, he is able to see far ahead and pay attention to detail.

A rational thinker and realist, intellectually independent he does not readily conform to convention. He shows a strong authoritative personality, one difficult to influence, not liking interference, with some aggressive and critical tendencies. He is a person capable of facing up to and overcoming difficulties.

He is materialistic with good business sense, well able to handle financial affairs and has good organizing ability. His behaviour is fairly consistent with a medium degree of adaptability in mind and behaviour.

There is a warm, generous side to the writer's personality showing consideration and a willingness to help and protect others. Although of a reserved and independent disposition there appears an underlying desire to be thought of as more outgoing. At times he may experience feelings of loneliness and when in company may show some social excitability as well as reticence. There are signs of strain and restrictive influences which are more than likely holding the writer back from a more relaxed attitude.

The writer holds a good opinion of himself, is ambitious and enthusiastic but there appears to be some uncertainty and restlessness with a tendency to change interests or end relationships abruptly in an endeavour to establish a firm purpose in life. He appears cautious in his actions, tending to procrastinate with some inner need to prepare himself before undertaking a job. He enjoys his creature comforts.

12. Samples of Handwriting for Analysis

Having studied the full analysis of Specimen 1 analyse the following eight specimens of handwriting by examining each feature individually, then after drawing up a Quality — Evidence Sheet correlate the salient qualities to form a character 'portrait' of the writer. (Note: samples have been reduced in size.)

For each specimen of handwriting the writer's age and sex is given below:

2.	Female	age 35 years.
3.	Male	late 60s.
4.	Female	age 33 years.
5.	Female	early 60s.
6.	Female	early 30s.
7.	Female	age 43 years.
8.	Female	age 37 years.
9.	Male	age 42 years.
10.	Female	age 70 years.

I was sorry to hear about your David. How is he coping with the idea of being pensioned off early? It really is a pity.

I'm glad that you're still enjoying your nursing. You're worrying about being a staff nurse but as you say there's still quite a time to go before that happens by which time I'm sure you'll be feeling a lot more confident.

The Kitten sounds lovely. I'm sure she'll be better than your other two in that she'll be a

A few days ago I encountered a friend of long standing whom I had not seen for many months. We met, as usual, near the local swimming baths as she, when in the vicinity, was an early swimmer and I an early shopper. She said that she had spent over a year practising (she was a doctor) in Thailand, but had to return home suddenly as her house there had been burned down and she had lost all her belongings taken there.

Ernest.

Sadie's two fat puppies continue to grow. They have legs like little tree trunks. One has always been bigger and fatter than the other, this is Bess or Bessie . The thinner one is Lizzie (Here is a pun you won't understand, there used to be a pop group called 'Thin Lizzie') But whoever gets them may rename them . A number of people are interested.

I hope the shop sale is going all right you must keep me informed. I also hope that my esteemed and aged father is keeping well. One way or another we will see you both this year.

Anyway take care in the meantime .

Lots of love

Ellen xxx

It was her first attempt at a Scottish poem, so she did exceptionally well.

I ~~must~~ go and post this while it is still daylight. Darkness comes down so early. Maybe I'll manage a little walk.

By the way, there was a nine week old border collie on offer to a good home when I was in Newtonmore and I found it very difficult to resist the temptation.

Hope you are both well. Take Care.

Love Agnes,

Dear Mum & Dad,

When I spoke to Dad on the 'phone recently I mentioned that Huw had drawn a picture of Popeye. Dad said he would like one, so I am enclosing one herewith. Interesting to note that he had drawn it and not traced it.

I am also enclosing a photograph of Huw & Louisa that that they had taken at school. I hope you like them

The Children & I went with the school on a coach to see "The Selfish Shellfish" at the Sadlers Wells Theatre last Saturday. They seemed to enjoy it although I found it just a pleasant escape from housework. We came back via "The Lights" which I hadn't seen before and found well worth the detour.

I hope you can make it on 14th January. We will in any event come up & see you before Christmas.

Love George

50 members on the books, but unfortunately only around 20/25 attend the meetings. We meet every first Wednesday in the month at the community centre, to have talks, demonstrations, etc. The fortnight in between we meet at members houses for clothes, silver and pottery parties, that sort of thing. Profits going to the Club. We also have outings to Historic Houses, Gardens and shows, plus our annual Dinner. We enter a float for the Gravelings Gala and have a stall. Our committee meetings are held monthly, usually ending with coffee and a large piece of home made cake!

Hope the above information is of interest, and look forward to seeing you on 6th May.

Sample 7

Inner city decay cannot be denied; it is aggressively visual in many of our major cities. Nevertheless, little forward thinking appears to be taking place when it comes to rural town and village development, especially in the further reaches of commuter country. Rural areas, despite overall planning schemes, risk becoming the hotch potch of quick financial return jerry building destined to become the embarrassment of the twenty-first century. This satisfies the immoral aspirations of only two sectors of society. First it provides power and wealth to already powerful and wealthy building companies whose reasons for raping our natural heritage are thinly disguised as heritage rescue. Second it offers a bastardized rural domestic environment to long haul commuters whose 'green wellies' image of country living — inspired by a plethora of rustic bliss glossy magazines — distorts what in fact is merely dormitory existence.

Pat Elliott

Sample 8

There is always a simple answer to every problem, unfortunately its always the wrong one.

R. Feynman

in my left eye + I am getting
the better of the infection in
the right socket.

I om very sad about mrs.
mushman. We shall all miss
her.

Thank you for all your
prayers for me.

Yours affectionately

holly.

Sample 10

13. Influence of State of Health on Handwriting

In the preceding chapters emphasis has been given to traits in handwriting which reveal the writer's inherent characteristics. Excessive alcohol, taking drugs, stress and the state of mental and physical health at the time of writing can also influence and be detected in handwriting.

Alcoholism

Alcohol taken in moderation is not an evil, in fact the occasional drink amongst friends and as a help in relaxing after a tiring day can be beneficial. The danger lies when this procedure becomes a harmful habit difficult to control.

The high level of stress in many forms of employment today, matrimonial problems, loneliness, a misguided sense of social enjoyment, frustrations and an already disturbed personality are amongst the many and varied causes of heavy drinking.

As a person's behaviour changes under the influence of drink showing slurred speech, unsteady gait and difficulty in picking up and holding objects, handwriting is likewise affected, the movements being less regulated due to impaired concentration and muscular control.

The writing of alcoholics can show:
Tremor and weak strokes.
Increased number of spelling mistakes and amendments.
Variable and heavier pressure.
Writing slightly larger; varying in height and width.
Uneven direction of lines.
Fluctuating slant or to the left.
Writing indistinct and smeary.

Although alcohol affects the behaviour of different people in different ways research has shown that there is a distinct pattern in handwriting changes under the influence of drink. These changes are best observed, when possible, by comparing the specimen of handwriting with one written when not influenced by alcohol.

Drug Addiction

Drug addiction is now a major problem world-wide. Like alcoholism taking drugs can affect the behaviour of different people differently, depending on the drug and to a certain extent the individual's circumstances and inherent qualities.

Addiction to drugs can bring a multitude of other problems: loss of job, ruining the individual's life, marriage breakup, theft in order to purchase drugs, loneliness, homelessness and sometimes death unless help is sought to fight the addiction.

Under the influence of drugs a person can become mentally confused, lack motivation and drive, suffer hallucinations, become self-centred with an inflated opinion of their own importance and show insubordination to others. Accordingly the writing of drug addicts can show:
Large writing
Irregularity and carelessly formed letters.
Slow speed with breaks in connections.
Muddled spacing between lines and words.
Inflated loops and Capital I as a personal pronoun.
Flourishes and exaggerated capitals.

Fluctuating slant and illegibility.
Heavy or variable pressure.

Signs of Stress

When undergoing excessive physical and/or mental strain chemical changes take place in our muscles causing fatigue. This is the body's way of warning us that rest is necessary before stress levels become too high with more serious consequences. Under stress handwriting shows less muscular control indicating the need to pause for rest as shown below:

1. In connections between letters within, or at the end of a word. Where in normal writing the forms of connection are clear and legible under stressful conditions, at irregular intervals, these letters degenerate into an illegible thread, written with lighter pressure. See Figure 65.

Figure 65

2. Loss of pressure is also noticeable in some starting and ending strokes sporadically throughout the script. See Figure 66.

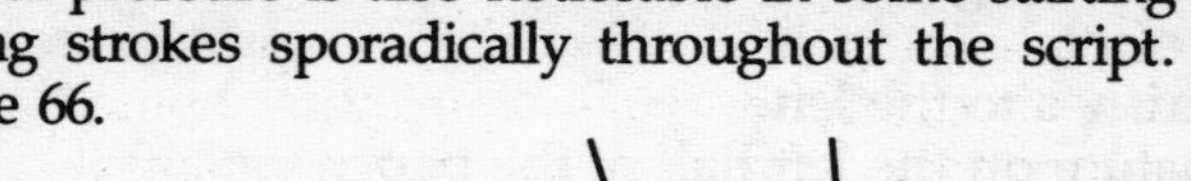

Figure 66

3. Breaks in the down-strokes of some letters, not present in normal writing, are another indication of stress due to reduced muscular control. See Figure 67.

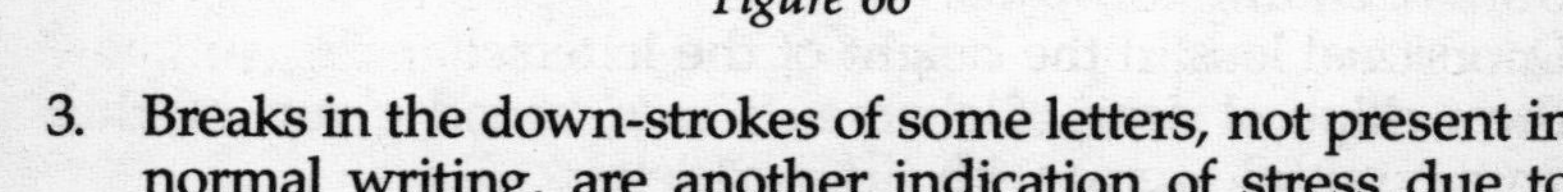

Figure 67

4.   Resting dots, blobs formed at the start and/or end of letters
     where the pen has rested over-long can indicate fatigue. The
     time taken in hesitating to form these dots is so short that
     the writer is usually unaware of their presence at the time
     of writing. See Figure 68.

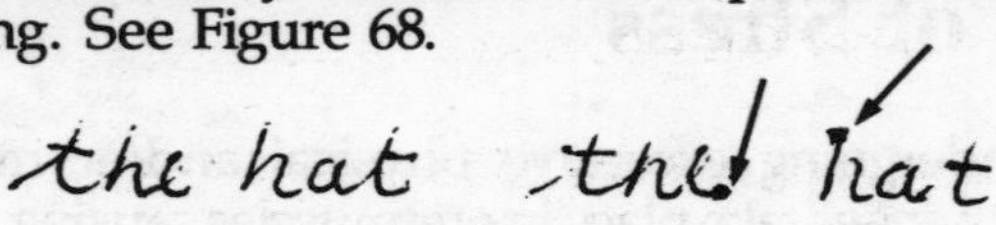

Figure 68

Indications of strain in handwriting such as these may be the
means of revealing the condition before it becomes critical.

Anxiety

Some writing characteristics of those suffering from anxiety, a
state of unwarranted fears and apprehensions usually
accompanied by restlessness, sleep disturbance and headaches,
are listed below:

Left placement of the script.
Lines starting to the left without a margin.
Left slant.
Flourishes to the left.
Signature on the left half of the paper.
Narrow spacing between lines and words.
Small writing.
Abrupt ending to words.
Occasional loss in the height of the letters.
Some elliptical forms of letters such as 'o', 'a' and 'g' run together
(in the middle zero) with the next letter.
Heavy pressure expressing 'heaviness of spirit' rather than
forcefulness or irregular loss of pressure.

Depression

Depressed people also have a tendency to show left placement of their script, a slant to the left and their signature to the left side of the paper. Other writing characteristics are shown below:

Descending lines or lines failing to reach the right side of the paper.
Small letters.
Capitals diminishing in size.
Amendments.
Slow writing.
Heavy pressure indicating 'heaviness of spirit' rather than forcefulness, irregular or weak frail pressure.

APPENDIX: Qualities — Characteristics Quick Reference Guide

Quality	Characteristics
Ability to stand up to stress	Slant upright, strong pressure, regular writing, angular connections, few or no left tendencies, stable baseline, high form level, firm t-bars, no large loops, knots in 't', 'f' and 'k', good connection, lines and words well-spaced, speed, i-dots over the stem.
Ability to get on with people	Right slant, garland connections, wide middle zone.
Abruptness in ending relationships	End strokes curtailed.
Absent-mindedness	i-dots and/or t-bars missing.
Affection	Wide writing with right slant.
Aggression	t-bars sharpening at end, sharpening of loops, hooks, long initial strokes.
Altruism	Right slant, right tendencies, top strokes of letters such as

Quality	**Characteristics**
	capital 'F', 'T' covering the whole word, extended end strokes.
Ambition to attain a goal	Ascending lines, right slant, second stroke of letters such as 'K', 'R' shorter.
Ambition depending on good opinion and approval of others	Second pointed top of capital 'M' mounting.
Anxiety	Left placement, lines and words close together, abrupt ending to words, slow writing, small writing, signature may be to the left of the paper, slant and flourishes may be to the left, pressure is heavy or weak and irregular, ellipses of 'a', 'o', 'g' etc. compressed to the next letter, abrupt loss in height of some letters.
Arrogance	Tall capitals, capital 'M' descending.
Artistic temperament	Full pasty writing, arcade connections.
Attention to detail — accuracy	i-dots directly over the stem, small writing.
Avoiding responsibility	Arcade formation to the left at lower lengths of the letters 'g' and 'y'.
Balanced writing	Regular rhythmic writing with the height of the 3 zones in proportion.
Black spot in the past	Letters starting with a black spot extending to the left as in capital 'C'.

Quality	Characteristics
Bossiness	Wide t-bar resting on top of the stem, lower length of 'g' in angular formation (this is also a sign of domestic tyranny).
Brutality	t-bars thickening at the end, slow writing with heavy pressure.
Calculating mind	Capital 'C' written like a complicated 'e' with a straight line drawn up to the start of the curl in the 'C'.
Carelessness	i-dots and/or t-bars missing.
Cautiousness	i-dots and t-bars to the left of the stem, upright script, initial letters set apart from the rest of the word.
Clarity of thought	Simplified angular writing.
Clear penetrating mind	Lean upper zone, sharpening at the tip and base of the letters.
Concentrate, ability to	Simplified writing, small and narrow, with no loops in the lower zone.
Consideration	Legible writing with good spacing.
Decisions, difficulty in making	Fluctuating slant throughout the script, thready formations.
Defensive, on the	Strokes extending below the baseline.
Dependability	Upright script, stable baseline, 'a' and 'o' closed.

Quality	Characteristics
Depression	Left slant, fluctuating or failing lines, heavy or weak and irregular pressure, small writing, slow writing, capital letters diminishing in height, corrections, and the signature placed to the left of the paper.
Desire to impress — call for attention	Initial letters larger than the rest of the word, elaborated capitals, flourishes and superflous strokes, and a flamboyant signature.
Diligence	Right slant, large starting strokes.
Diplomacy	Arcade connections, words and capitals diminishing in size, some threads, 'a' and 'o' closed.
Disappointment	End strokes dropping below the baseline.
Dishonesty	Base of 'a', 'o' and 'd' open.
Dislikes interference	Angular formations in the lower zone, angular t-bars.
Distrust	Covering strokes, narrow writing.
Dreamer	Large inflated loops in the upper zone, t-bars well above the stem.
Ego, inflated	Exaggerated capitals, inflated 'I' as a personal pronoun, enrolment.
Egotism	Left slant and tendencies, enrolment.

Quality	Characteristics
Emotional instability	Uneven baseline, conflicting slants, fluctuating size of letters, irregular spacing of words and lines, mingling, irregular pressure, sudden bursts of pressure.
Enjoys food and good living	Pasty writing, large writing, wide spacing between the letters.
Enthusiasm	Ascending lines, long t-bars to the right, large writing.
Excitability	Strong slope to the right, t-bars sloping upwards, heavy pressure, ascending lines, quick writing, initial letters with long rising strokes, sudden fullness of one letter formation throughout script.
Fighting spirit	Signs as of Aggression — hooks, sharpening of loops, t-bars sharpening at the end, t-bars pointing downwards, letter x as two crosses.
Flamboyance	See Desire to impress — inflated loops, exaggerated capitals etc.
Frankness	Stable baseline, 'a' and 'o' mostly open at the top, end of words rising.
Friendliness	As Ability to get on with people — right slant, garland connections, wide middle zone.

Quality	Characteristics
Good starter	No starting strokes, good layout.
Greed	Left tendencies, t-bars and the ends of words are formed like a 'grasping claw'.
Hastiness	i-dots in the form of a dash, t-bars to the right sometimes disconnected from the stem, quick writing.
Honesty	Simplification, regular writing with good speed, few or no left tendencies, high form level, legible writing, garland connections, letters in words increasing in size.
Idealism	The upper zone is dominant, t-bars over the stem.
Imagination, good	Large high loops in the upper zone, t-bars above the stem, full writing.
Indecision	Thready formations, fluctuating slant.
Independence	Upright writing, stable baseline, arcade connections, t-bars curving back and overhead.
Initiative, not willing to take	Initial letters smaller than the rest of the word.
Intelligence	Simplification, good layout, letters decreasing in size at the end of words, t-bars and i-dots connected to previous or following letter.

Quality	**Characteristic**
Introvert	Left slant.
Intuition	High form level, disconnected writing, pasty, full writing.
Isolation, sense of	Over-wide spacing between the lines and words, writing surrounded by wide margins.
Jealousy	Strong right slant, some small letters — often 'a' — exaggerated in size throughout the script.
Judgement, good	Well-connected, upright writing.
Kindness	Garland connections.
Leadership	Regular writing, large writing, strong pressure.
Logical thinker	Simplification, connected writing.
Loneliness	Lines and words are close together, strong slant to the right (needing people).
Malice	Small sharp writing.
Materialism	The lower zone is dominant, left tendencies, triangular base to lower loops.
Mechanical mind	Square letter formation.
Memory, good	Good connection, i-dots directly over the stem, carefully placed punctuation, good spacing between the lines and words.
Modesty	Small writing, small capitals.

Quality	Characteristics
Moodiness	Irregular writing, irregular direction of lines, the height of the middle zone is disproportionally small to the full length.
Muddle-headedness	Inflated loops in the upper zone, with t-bars high above the stem.
Musical	Letters are formed like musical notes.
Observation, good	i-dots are like 'watching eyes', there are breaks after capitals, disconnected writing.
Obstinacy	Hooks, the end-strokes drop below the baseline, angular writing, heavy pressure.
Obtrusive	Close spacing between words and lines, no paragraphs, mingling of letters between lines, very small or no margins.
Organizer, good	Lines and words are well-spaced, good layout, straight left margin, long lower lengths.
Originality	Original letter formation, irregular writing, disconnected writing.
Pessimism	Descending lines.
Pride in own or family achievements	t-bars formed into a rounded loop.
Procrastination	i-dots and t-bars to the left of the stem, initial letters

Quality	Characteristics
	standing apart from the rest of word, thread formations.
Patronizing, protection, sense of	The top stroke of letters such as capital 'T' extend to cover the whole word.
Quarrelsome	Long starting strokes beginning below the baseline, mingling, hooks, t-bars mounting, heavy pressure.
Realism, sense of	Upright writing, small, underlengths are dominant, disconnected writing.
Resentfulness	Small writing, lean, sharp, angular connections.
Reserve	Upright slant or a slant to the left, large spaces between words and lines, 'a' and 'o' closed.
Resilience	See Ability to stand up to stress.
Scientific mind	Simplification, i-dots and t-bars connected to the preceding or the following letter.
Self-admiration	The lower stroke of letters such as capital 'L' are underlining the word.
Self-confidence	Large, wide, quick writing:
Self confidence, lack of	Small writing, decending lines, weak pressure, a neglected middle zone, low t-bars, and slow writing.

Quality	**Characteristics**
Self-sacrifice, capable of	Right slant.
Sex — anxiety	Stunted lower lengths of 'g' and 'y'.
Sex — drive	Strong lower zone.
Sex — imagination	Inflated loops in lower lengths of 'g' and 'y'.
Sex — rejection of	The lower zone of 'g' and 'y' is short or absent.
Shyness	Narrow capitals.
Sincerity	Some 'a's' and 'o's' open, some closed, garland connections, wide writing, the letters in words increasing in size.
Social involvement, main interest	Large middle zone, disproportionally large compared with the full length.
Spender	Waste of space, poor layout, wide spacing between letters.
Steady worker	Regular writing.
Sticking to essentials, capable of	Simplified writing, no starting strokes.
Talkative	Wide writing, 'a' and 'o' wide open at the top.
Thoughts running ahead of actions	i-dots far to the right, t-bars to the right sometimes disconnected from the stem.
Tidiness	Good layout, margins regular, good spacing, the script of neat appearance.

Quality	Characteristics
Timidity	Light pressure, small writing, left slant.
Tiredness	Small writing, weak pressure, breaks in down-strokes, shaky strokes, lines descending, resting dots, letters degenerating into threads.
Toughness	Angular connections, knotted t-bars and knots in letters such as 'k'.
Unpretentious	Natural writing with no flourishes or superfluous strokes, the signature the same size and form as in the script.
Versatility	Mixture of connected and disconnected writing, several different formations e.g. in 'f', 's', 'y'.
Vitality	Large rhythmic writing, quick writing, strong even pressure.
Volatile personality	Fluctuating slants throughout the script. Garland connections, wide middle zone.
Warm personality	Garland connections, wide middle zone.
Will power, lacking in	Weak t-bars.

Suggested Titles for Further Reading

Analysis of Handwriting, H.J. Jacoby, George Allen and Unwin Ltd., 1939.

A Manual of Graphology, Eric Singer, Duckworth, 1969.

Man and His Symbols, Carl Jung, Aldus Books Ltd., 1964.

Graphology, Patricia Marne, Teach Yourself/Hodder and Stoughton, 1980.

Crime and Sex in Handwriting, Patricia Marne, Constable, 1981.

The Secret's in Their Signature, Patricia Marne, 1986.

What Your Handwriting Reveals, Margaret Gullan-Whur, Aquarian Press, 1984.

Index